01

02

TEACHING
ONE MOMENT
AT A TIME

TEACHING ONE MOMENT AT A TIME

Disruption and Repair in the Classroom

DAWN M. SKORCZEWSKI

University of Massachusetts Press   Amherst and Boston

LC 2004030734
ISBN 1-55849-495-2

Designed by Sally Nichols
Set in Monotype Goudy Modern
Printed and bound by The Maple-Vail Book Manufacturing Group

Library of Congress Cataloging-in-Publication Data

Skorczewski, Dawn M.
Teaching one moment at a time : disruption and repair in the classroom / Dawn M.
Skorczewski.
    p. cm.
Includes bibliographical references.
ISBN 1-55849-495-2 (cloth : alk. paper)
1. English language—Rhetoric—Study and teaching. 2. English language—
Composition and exercises—Study and teaching. 3. Report writing—Study
and teaching. 4. Teacher-student relationships. 5. Classroom environment. I.
Title.
PE1404.S59 2005
808'.042'071—dc22

2004030734

British Library Cataloguing in Publication data are available.

"This Much I Do Remember" from *Picnic, Lightning*, by Billy Collins,
© 1998. Reprinted by permission of the University of Pittsburgh Press.

"The Poems of Our Climate" from *The Collected Poems of Wallace Stevens*,
by Wallace Stevens, © 1954 by Wallace Stevens and renewed 1982 by
Holly Stevens. Used by permission of Alfred A. Knopf, a division of
Random House, Inc.

"What If God" from *The Gold Cell*, by Sharon Olds, © 1987 by Sharon
Olds. Used by permission of Alfred A. Knopf, a division of Random
House, Inc.

For Leni Herzog

*"For thy sweet love remembered such wealth brings
that then I'd scorn to change my state with kings"*

CONTENTS

ACKNOWLEDGMENTS

This book, years in the writing, is as much a tribute to co-creative processes as are the classes and interactions on which it is based. From the start, Kurt Spellmeyer, Hugh English, Richard E. Miller, Nancy Sommers, Rosemarie Bodenheimer, Maxine Rodburg, Ken Smith, Christy Jespersen, Lisa Marcus, Jim Albrecht, Linda Adler-Kassner, Susan Murray, and Paul Thur helped to formulate the basic concepts and encouraged me to take risks. The students at Rutgers University, the University of Redlands, Harvard University, and Emerson College inspired me to keep thinking about what we were creating together. Jeffrey Berman, Peter Elbow, Murray Schwartz, Clark Dougan, Nancy Raynor, and Carol Betsch provided invaluable advice about the publication of the manuscript. Dolan Power, Lisa and Joel Rubenstein, Dan Brenner, Maxine Alchek, and Jim Walton kept me moving toward useful applications of psychoanalysis. Ed Tronick, Marilyn Davillier, and Alexandra Harrison invented the theories that hold up the text and brought me to new mixtures of work and play. Clement Van Buren steered the book through the middle passages, leaving the Stevens poem of chapter 5 in his wake. Sharon Olds initiated the dialogue in chapter 5 and generously continues it to this day. Cara Crandall acted as example, editor, coach, and ally. Connie Richard, Kerry Monaghan, and Jessie Janeshek became tireless researchers, editors, and energy boosters. Lewis Kirshner lovingly roamed through the final manuscript to find the life of its argument. And every step of the way was easier because of the witty, curious, and supportive Matthew Parfitt, Wendy Walters, Ellen and David Rome, Tess Skorczewski, and Barrie Stevens.

Without them, as well as Leni Herzog's indefatigable dedication and vision, these ideas and their author would not have found a home. Finally, I thank the teachers at Emerson College. The stories in these pages, with all their wisdom, work, and passion, cannot do justice to what these people have taught me about teaching and learning, one moment at a time.

Earlier versions of portions of chapter 5 were previously published as "Questioning Authority in the Psychoanalytic Classroom," *Psychoanalytic Quarterly*, April 2004, 485–510, and "Whose Neighborhood Is This? Intersubjective Moments in Psychoanalytic Education," *PsyArt: An Online Journal for the Psychological Study of the Arts*, June 2002, http://www.clas.ufl.edu/ipsa/journal/. An earlier version of chapter 3 previously appeared in *College Composition and Communication*, December 2000, 220–39. I am grateful to the editors for permission to reuse this material here.

TEACHING
ONE MOMENT
AT A TIME

TEACHING ONE MOMENT AT A TIME
Disruption and Repair in the Classroom

All the moments of the past
Began to line up behind that moment
And all the moments to come
Assembled in front of it in a long row,
Giving me reason to believe
That this was a moment I had rescued
From the millions that rush out of sight
Into a darkness behind the eyes.

Even after I have forgotten what year it is,
My middle name,
And the meaning of money,
I will carry in my pocket
The small coin of that moment,
Minted in the kingdom
That we pace through every day.

—Billy Collins, "This Much I Do Remember"

I INVITE YOU TO JOURNEY BACK EIGHTEEN YEARS WITH ME AS I walk into a classroom for the very first time as the teacher. Armed with the syllabus and copies of the poem that I will distribute, I look in the door, note the students seated around the room, enter the classroom, and proceed to the front. I feel myself walk to the teacher's desk and place my brand new briefcase and mimeographed, ink-smelling handouts on it. I hear myself say my name and the name of the course. I smile. A student in the second row smiles back at me. In a split second, I am interpreting her smile. It seems to say to me, "I am excited to be in my first college writing course and happy that you will be my teacher." Her smile results, perhaps, from her sense of what I am communicating to her: "You are my very first group of students. I am your teacher. I am looking forward to working together." I feel my legs and shoulders begin to relax, and for a moment I gain access to the excitement about teaching that I had nurtured for years. The student's warm smile gives me a surge of confidence. I will now shape fifty minutes of time in this classroom into something that my students and I will call a "writing class." Over and over in those fifty minutes, in innumerable ways, I will communicate to my students: "I am your teacher; you are my students; we will be learning together, and here is what that will mean."

Although research in the teaching of writing is filled with examples of moments such as the one that I have just described, we do not often attempt to conceptualize in any detail the millions of minute interactions between students and teachers that constitute what we call a "class." During these moments, we articulate, both directly and indirectly, what it means to us to be teachers, how we perceive our students, and how we interpret the interactions between us: "This is who I am; this is who you are; this is who we are together, right now."

Classrooms are dynamic places; our conversations, both written and spoken, rapidly shift, in constant flux. Teachers know this about teaching, and they develop methods to shape their interactions with students. The shapes of these interactions in various ways reflect the relational component of their pedagogical theories, a component which becomes so natural that it can seem to be common sense. "Of course we smile and look our students in the eye on the first day," we might say. "How else can you be a teacher?" Yet any of us could offer an example of a teacher who does not behave this way. And if we spoke to such a teacher, we might find that smiling is not something on the list of pedagogical tools to be used in his or her classroom. We might also know of a teacher who does not smile but has an engaging look, a teacher whose body language says to students, "I am 100 percent here and ready to work. Are you?" All teachers, regardless of when and how much they smile, experience frustrating silences in the classroom or seemingly passive, unmotivated, or confrontational students. These students' responses often reflect something about their teachers' ways of being with them. Knowledge about these ways of being remains outside teachers' awareness, because their focus is often the students and the material. The least visible thing to the teacher is, of course, the teacher him- or herself.

In the field of composition, attention has turned increasingly to situated and local accounts of classroom experience as sources of knowledge. It is common to ask, for example, how students' life experiences shape their experiences in writing classrooms, how race, class, gender, sexuality, and ethnicity figure in the construction of writing. We can find many studies of individual students' and teachers' experiences in particular writing classes (Berman, *Diaries;* Herrington; Sommers; Sternglass; Trimmer), as well as narratives of teachers' attempts to understand their students in ways other than those traditionally available to us. In a review of affective approaches to the teaching of writing, Richard Fulkerson asks what a course might look like when we attend to the noncognitive aspects of teaching. Richard E. Miller calls these noncognitive approaches "the arts of engagement" (*As If Learning Mattered* 21), whereas Eugene Gendlin and Sondra Perl use the term "felt sense" (Gendlin 17–19; Perl 151). Kurt Spellmeyer refers to this felt sense when he urges us to become what he calls "ethnographers of experience: scholar/teachers who find out how people actually *feel* . . . [who] search for basic grammars of emotional life" (*Common Ground* 242).

It would make sense that teachers of writing would have a lot to say about students and teachers as emotional beings in the classroom. After all, we have been talking about personal experiences in the teaching of writing for almost three decades. Joseph Harris traces the development of the "growth" model of teaching writing to the three-week Seminar on the Teaching and Learning of English at Dartmouth College (the Dartmouth Seminar) in 1966, which fostered the belief that writing raises the issue of "felt experience" in a way that perhaps no other discipline does. Experience-based models of writing instruction thrived in the seventies and eighties (Elbow; Murray; Newkirk; Joseph Harris; Tobin). Ethnographies of teaching also began to appear in these decades, as expert teachers and researchers argued that teachers and their students should study what happens in actual classrooms as a source of knowledge (Branscombe, Goswami, and Schwartz; Schon). And although constructionist and postprocess models have directed attention away from personal writing in more-recent years, composition theorists remain interested in realms of experience, including those of embodied students and teachers (Fleikenstein; Hesse; Jacobs; Prendergast).

Despite this wonderful research, much remains to be discovered about the teacher's embodied experiences and unconscious expressions of what it feels like to be the instructor in the writing class. What can we discover about an instructor's ways of being in a particular course at a specific moment in time, and what is to be gained from this knowledge? How does a teacher's experience of students' reactions to him or her in a given moment shape what happens next? Many of the writers I cite move us toward an understanding of the dance, or dialogue, of affective exchanges that is a part of every successful teaching experience. They do not for the most part, however, address the teacher as a subject in this dialogue from one moment to the next.

Richard G. Tiberius and Jane Tipping, researchers in the field of medical education, begin to think about teachers as actors in the emotional world of the classroom when they distinguish between cognitive functions in the classroom discussion and relational issues. They consider the difference between "work-oriented functions . . . such as clarifying the topic and maintaining focus, and . . . process-oriented functions . . . that indirectly support the learning objectives, such as maintaining and encouraging a safe and comfortable psychological climate" (110). To build, maintain, and encourage a "safe and comfortable psychological climate" in the classroom, they suggest, we need to attend to an aspect of pedagogy very different from those addressed in many of our courses in and conversations about teaching.

In this book, I examine a number of stories about teaching to consider the teacher's contribution to the back-and-forth exchanges of meaning, both verbal and nonverbal, that make up the split-second world of the class. The stories include encounters from my life as a writing teacher and program director during more than a decade of writing program administration. They include stories of the students I have taught in graduate courses in the teaching of writing, the teachers I supervise in my role as director of composition, and the friends and colleagues with whom I have discussed teaching over the years. The stories trace teachers' ways of being in classrooms as they echo back through the comments and the written work of students. In telling these stories I hope not only to speak in detail about classroom interactions but also to offer a perspective on teaching that is prompted by the response of the students *to* the teacher, rather than the analysis *of* the students *by* the teacher. The teacher is in some sense both the subject and the object of inquiry in this book.

I have chosen the concept of "the moment" as the locus for this investigation of teachers' ways of being in the classroom to evoke different disciplinary and generic conceptions of "being together in time" that are in my mind when I talk about teaching. In a moment, we can smile at a group of students, snap at them, seize their imaginations, or lull them to sleep. In a moment, we create a feeling of possibility in the room or close it down. The concept of the moment is common in Buddhist formulations of being in this place at this time. It also occurs in dozens of poems in which the speakers call us to be present with them in a particular place with its concomitant feelings. The Billy Collins poem that is the epigraph to this introduction, for example, invites one into the regal and the mundane moment of the "kingdom / That we pace through every day." Collins's speaker brings to mind other literary representations of the moment, such as Virginia Woolf's "moments of being," William Wordsworth's "spots of time" in *The Prelude,* or T. S. Eliot's "in a moment there is time for decisions and revisions which a moment will erase" from his "Love Song of J. Alfred Prufrock." The concept of "the moment" is also common in psychoanalytic and psychological discourses with which I have become familiar, as when infant researchers talk about "the split-second world" or psychoanalysts in the Boston Process of Change Study Group describe "now moments" (Stern et al.).

Teaching One Moment at a Time examines dozens of "moments" in the classroom when business as usual is either disrupted or thrown into relief by circumstances that are rather unusual. Students who seem compelled to use clichés despite their instructor's advice that they not; a young teacher who is repeatedly accused of being unable to listen to her students; a seasoned instructor who is first screamed at and then cried to in her office—these are examples of times when teachers are best positioned to see their own roles in what is so easy to mistake as simply students' disruptions or subversions of the goals of the course. It might be tempting, for example, to view the clichés of our students as evidence of their limited cultural vocabulary and educational preparation, their need for ways of understanding the world that go beyond what they conceive of as common sense. But might a teacher's response to students' clichés assume a clichéd pattern as well and indicate the common sense of the instructor, who has been trained to eschew cliché as somehow beyond the realm of critical thinking?

A teacher's most difficult or vexing interactions with students provide excellent vantage points from which teachers can examine their own, often unconscious participation in the construction of knowledge in courses. Any interpretation of what students say or do in oral or written conversation with us reflects a delicate negotiation between what our training and experiences have prepared us to hear and what a student is trying to, or learning to, articulate. The premise of this book is that the teacher who recognizes the assumptions he or she brings to these conversations is equipped to listen to students more carefully than the teacher who understands his or her assumptions as common sense.

We need to look no further than the places that most offend, frustrate, or annoy us in student writing to find clues for how to read our personal ideology as it presents itself in response to our students' work. A graduate student instructor who hands out a list of pet peeves at the beginning of the semester might not realize the extent to which personal taste is shaping what gets called "effective writing" in the classroom. No less significant, but far more subtle, is a seasoned instructor's valuing or devaluing of students' contributions to a discussion of a course text. In these instances, a nod of the head can indicate who is on track and who is off; the instructor names what the track is and where the discussion will go. We cannot avoid this, but we can recognize it, although the act of recognition is far more difficult than it might at first appear.

The best indicators of an instructor's implicit ways of being in the classroom, if we can bear to examine them, exist in responses to situations that seem most difficult. In difficult situations, we teach in an atmosphere of risk and danger, at the edge of what we have experienced and the threshold of who we are becoming as teachers. Many of us became teachers because we enjoy generating ideas with students in a lively classroom environment. We are drawn to the risky scene even as we fear what might happen in such an environment, where each decision we make can feel critical to the progress of the class and to our success or failure as a teacher.

In each chapter of this book, I isolate a challenging situation for any teacher and tell the stories of teachers, including myself, who experience its complexities: becoming a teacher, leading discussions, designing assignments, responding to student writing, negotiating authority, and making self-disclosures in the classroom. In each case, I identify the moment, tease out a number of possible interpretations of it, and then attempt to understand what these interpretations teach us about the interpreters themselves. Although any one of us knows how to "get by" as a teacher in the situations I describe, many of these teachers actually confronted these situations as opportunities to grow as teachers and human beings.

My search for a language to capture the lessons of the difficult moments I describe led me to accept an appointment as an affiliate scholar at the Boston Psychoanalytic Society and Institute, where I enrolled in courses in which I was exposed to psychoanalytic models of interaction that I had not previously encountered. My familiarity with analysis at that point was limited to a standard Freudian model, a cursory reading of Lacan, and a few postmodern analytic tropes that seemed to have little relevance to the classrooms I knew. To make sense of the "local level" (Stern et al. 904) of interaction at various moments in the teaching process, I struggled to integrate terms and ideas from recent psychoanalytic theory, nonlinear dynamic systems theory, and infant research. Terms and concepts from these disciplines have helped me to tease out the ways in which interactions between students and teachers are influenced by the subjectivity of writing instructors. Looking outside our own discipline, we see ourselves from new perspectives, uncover the teacher's presence in the classroom from another angle, and expand the possibilities of how we interact with our students in the future.

Research in the teaching of writing has referred with some frequency to classical Freudian and Lacanian models of psychoanalysis as key to understanding our interactions with students (Berman, *Diaries*; Bracher; Finke; Jay; Tobin). Much of this research discusses the student writer as an individual trapped in unconscious conflicts that interfere with or adversely influence the writing process. In this literature, students are often imagined as people who may be cured or liberated by their instructors, people who cannot see the conflicts that embroil them because they are too close to them. Writing instructors, on the outside of the conflicts students face in the writing process, are depicted as trained, self-possessed professionals who are positioned to help. But these theories do not consider in much detail what a teacher brings to the interpersonal domain of the writing course without the explicit knowledge that it is there, a very important aspect of the relational world of the writing classroom.

As they are typically applied to teaching, Freudian and Lacanian models do not address the critical and personal lenses through which writing instructors (often unconsciously) do their work. Sifting through a number of psychoanalytic approaches to the writing classroom, I attempt to establish that seeing the classroom as a space for teachers to unlock the psyches of their students elides both the experiences of the teachers and, ironically, those of the students themselves. Unlike their teachers, who often conceive of themselves as offering new forms of knowledge to their students, students sometimes suggest that they are subjected to ways of thinking and being that are unfamiliar and even threatening to them, ways of being and thinking that undercut or stifle the development of their ideas. Becoming more aware of our own roles in the shaping of knowledge in our classrooms may help us to promote the growth of our students more than any attempts to heal or liberate them that originate from overconfidence in our expertise.

Admittedly, Freudian and Lacanian models might be as useful in understanding the unconscious conflicts that teachers bring into the writing classroom as they are in exploring the students' conflicts; some work in our field has begun to explore this domain (see especially Tobin). I draw primarily from a different body of research to explore a more interpersonal aspect of the instructor's role in the writing course. Freudian and Lacanian models focus largely on the internal world, the unconscious conflictual realm of the individual subject. More recent publications in psychoanalysis, dynamic systems theory, and infant research direct attention to what is called the "intersubjective realm," the interpersonal world in which individuals build understanding through their subjective experiences of what is happening between them.

An intersubjective exchange would, for example, involve a mutual experience of recognition of the other's motives, desires, and implicit goals, as well as the feelings that accompany this process (Beebe and Lachmann 216; Tronick et al.). This sharing might be thought to articulate "I know what you are thinking, and you know what I am thinking." Thomas Cottle speaks of intersubjective understanding, or "mutual otherness," as key to identity formation and learning; all "teaching," by definition, occurs within the relationship, within the connection of our mutual otherness, and thus it lives in a remarkable zone conjoining the physical and metaphysical worlds (69). When considered in relationship to the writing classroom, in which as many as thirty students interact with their teacher, the course texts, and each other, the potential for intersubjective meetings both multiplies and shrinks by virtue of the sheer number of opportunities for connection and disruption.

Infant researchers add a very important element to our understanding of the intersubjective component of classroom interactions in their focus on what is called the "split-second world" (Beebe and

Stern). These researchers use videotaped sessions between primary caregivers and their children to determine how the infant and parent respond to each other from moment to moment, drawing each other into interactions that contain both meaning and intention. Infant researcher Louis Sander describes this videotaped sequence of a father and his infant:

> Frame-by-frame, one sees the father glance down momentarily at the baby's face. Strangely enough, in the same frames, the infant looks up at the father's face. Then the infant's left arm, which had been hanging down over the father's left arm, begins to move upward. Miraculously, in the same frame, the father's right arm, which had been hanging down at his right side, begins to move upward. Frame by frame by frame, the baby's hand and the father's hand move upward simultaneously. Finally, just as they meet over the baby's tummy, the baby's left hand grasps the little finger of the father's right hand. At that moment, the infant's eyes close and she falls asleep, while father continues talking, apparently totally unaware of the little miracle of specificity in time, place, and movement that had taken place in his arms. (Sander, "Thinking Differently" 20)

The "little miracle of specificity" that occurs between this father and infant is in part such a miracle because it is simultaneous: initiated neither by the father nor the infant, but mutually created. The child does not, for example, mirror or mimic his father; nor does the father attempt to coax the child into engagement. Instead, the two respond to each other in a dance of relatedness, a dance that is accessible to us only because Sander captures it on tape. This "little miracle of specificity" is by no means limited to the first year of life. The rhythms of connection and disconnection between students and teachers in classrooms occur in similar and equally hard-to-capture ways.

Infant researchers study verbal and nonverbal dimensions of relationships between the youngest human beings and their parents, and yet these researchers' attention to what they call the "local level" and the "split-second world" of human relationships has much to offer those of us who attempt to understand what happens in classrooms. In the "split-second world" of the "local level," a group of talkative students becomes suddenly silent, or sullen and seemingly passive students come to life. Like the father and infant above, students and teachers participate in a nonverbal coordination or discoordination in these moments, but unlike the father and infant, they also exchange meanings on the verbal or symbolic level. I attempt to look at both the nonverbal and verbal exchanges—sometimes separately, as in the design of an assignment or a student's response to it, and sometimes simultaneously, as in a teacher's encounter with a difficult student—with an interest in discovering how the nonverbal dimension contributes to the making of meaning in the symbolic realm.

When we attend to the nonverbal world of teaching, we begin to see the actions that bring about a behavioral "fittedness" between the people in a classroom (Sander, "Regulation of Exchange" 139). Fittedness might include positioning of the students and teacher, coupled with the facial and verbal stimulation of both instructors and students during discussions. It can refer to the falling and rising of voices, the intonation used when a teacher addresses a chronically late student, or the affirming nod when a bright student makes a particularly insightful remark. It can also be used to describe the way a disaffected student turns his body away from the group in the discussion, or the barely controlled rage expressed in the rolled eyes of a student whose teacher muses about how unfortunate it is that his computer crashed for the fourth time in one semester. The teacher's overtures and responses to students contribute to the ebb and flow of fittedness as much as the students themselves.

The ways in which the instructor monitors his or her fittedness with the students in a class discussion, a writing conference, or a chat in the hallway can be explored through the concepts of self- and interactive regulation from infant research (Beebe and Lachmann 216). The teacher actively compares what she is observing in herself with what she believes is happening in her students' minds. A process of checking in, which is often very subtle, can verify whether the teacher is correct in assuming that students are bored, for example, or restless or confused. The teacher compares these observations with what he or she is feeling inside, to gauge where to take the group next or how to respond to a particular question or challenge. Beebe and Lachmann suggest "that the expectation of being matched, as well as the expectation of matching and participating in the state of the other," or of being "on the same wavelength," is central to human development. As infants, we internalize both the experience of "I reflect you" and "I change with you. We are going in the same direction. I experience myself as tracking and being tracked by you" (216).

When the teacher senses that something which needs to happen is not happening, or the reverse, infant researchers believe a "mismatch" or "disruption" has occurred. In infant research, mismatches are not unfortunate or to be avoided but part of healthy development: "The typical mother-infant interaction moves from coordinated to mis-coordinated states and back again over a wide affective range. . . . Mis-communications are normal events. They occur when one of the part-ners fails to accurately appreciate the meaning of the other's emotion-al display and in turn reacts inappropriately. . . . Given that the infant and mother are active regulators of each other's behavior, the process of reparation also is a mutually regulated process" (Tronick et al. 294).

Disruption and repair, or mismatch and reparation, is a central con-cept in this book. We make a mistake, misjudge or misunderstand our students, or they misinterpret or misunderstand us. Once we recognize what is happening, we attempt to repair the situation by doing some-thing differently or by figuring out what the problem was in conversa-tions with our students. It is important to realize that disruption and repair are not about fixing broken classes or solving problems with solu-tions that can be enacted in an instant but a process through which stu-dents and teachers lose and refind each other and themselves over and over again. The teacher who embraces this process takes numerous risks and realizes the rewards of deep engagement with her or his students.

The principle of disruption and repair describes classroom experi-ence as organized by alternations between optimal fittedness and con-trast, disjunction, and difference. A classroom in which the fit between the teacher and a group of students generally feels good will necessarily also involve innumerable instances when the fit does not feel good, instances of disruption and the possibility for repair. In such an environment, the gap between what is expected and what is happening can be addressed and the fit reestablished. Infant researchers Beebe and Lachmann observe that "optimally coordinated regulations organize experiences of coherence, predictability, fitting together with the partner, and being well-related. The expectation develops that it is possible for the coordination to be sustained. . . . [T]he firmer the expectation that coordination can be sustained, the better the [person] will be able to tolerate and benefit from experiences of disruption and repair" (169). When they are too frequent, disruptions become the norm, and a class can become stuck: "In normal circumstances the sloppiness of the co-creative process prevents meaning from becoming fixed. Fixedness . . . prevents change and growth and even may be a feature of pathological relationships" (Tronick 477). Few of the classrooms I will describe in this book have become fixed; instead, they are lively places in which students and teachers regularly misunderstand or miss each other and engage in acts of repair.

"Intersubjectivity," "the split-second world," "the local level," "fittedness," "self- and mutual regulation," and "disruption and repair" are a few of the key terms from psychoanalysis and infant research that help us to explore the teacher's implicit relational patterns in the classroom. In the chapters that follow, I explore these patterns as they are revealed in students' responses to teachers, whether in written form or, more typically, in verbal exchanges, at every stage of the writing process. But I also focus on essential phases in the teaching of any discipline, from inhabiting the position of teacher in the classroom to responding to student writing, to confronting challenges to the teacher's authority.

In bringing the discourses of human development, psychology, and nonlinear dynamic systems theory into contact with teaching, I hope to establish a model for thinking about classroom interactions that is at once metaphorical and literal. Teachers are not parents working with young infants, and yet those who do work with infants have much to offer us in their analyses of how infants co-create understandings of themselves and the world with their parents (see especially Tronick). Nor are we psychoanalysts, who attempt to help analysands articulate, interpret, and understand their internal and interpersonal worlds. But like analysts, we are in the business of helping others "destroy old structures and create new ones," and in doing so, we must be willing to destroy and reconstruct ourselves (Stechler, quoted in Waters 2). We are, of course, human beings with our own psychological and developmental histories and conflicts, and however conscious they may be, these histories and conflicts deeply influence the ways our students experience us and the classes that we teach. Bringing these aspects of teaching into consciousness has, for me, been one of the most liberating parts of the process of becoming a successful teacher and program director.

Although in this book I address essential moments in the development of a writing instructor, I might as easily describe the development of an instructor of almost any college course in which writing is a component. The development of one's identity as teacher and leader of successful class discussions, the subjects of chapters 1 and 2, poses a challenge in any discipline. Likewise, designing assignments and responding to student writing, the topics of chapters 3 and 4, are common to most college courses. In chapter 5, which concerns negotiating authority in classrooms at a psychoanalytic institute, readers from every discipline are invited to imagine how the issues raised there might inform their teaching. Finally, in chapter 6, I discuss how a teacher might make use of the personal details of his or her life to expand the capacity for play in the classroom. When the classroom becomes a creative space in which definitions of what it means to teach are produced, interrogated, and replaced by others, it becomes more exciting and productive for teachres and students. And when those in charge embrace rather than exile the most difficult personal, social, and institutional questions, a classroom also becomes a site for transformation.

CHAPTER ONE

FROM PLAYING THE ROLE TO BEING YOURSELF

Becoming the Teacher in the Writing Classroom

The situation most pregnant with the possibility for
change is a system poised on the edge of chaos.

—Esther Thelen and Linda B. Smith,
*A Dynamic Systems Approach
to the Development of Cognition and Action*

IT WAS THE END OF HER THIRD DAY OF TEACHING, AND SHE COULD
not wait to leave the campus. Although she had settled into the idea
of being a teacher in a classroom on the first day and had led what
she thought was a productive class discussion on the second, the next
part of the task, to keep it going, was not working. She was unable to
move the discussion forward. There were uncomfortable silences into
which she inserted seemingly inconsequential information. A sea of
blank faces stared at her in response to more than half the questions
she asked. In addition, she found herself asserting authority over her
students in the most banal ways: almost shouting at them as she told

them they needed to speak if they were to have a productive discussion, irritated that one of the students was late for the second day in a row, and anxious that her mentor teacher would come visit the class and see her as the fraud that she knew she was. Her deepest fears about herself were surging to the surface. The worst part was that she could not talk about it with anyone she knew because they would then see that she was not qualified to teach the class.

When I first had these experiences eighteen years ago, I thought that I was alone in my fears of being an impostor rather than the teacher in a writing classroom. In the intervening years, as I moved from the position of writing instructor to director of composition, my fears have been echoed by dozens of teachers I have supervised. In my conversations with these teachers, I have tried to help them find ways of being themselves while maintaining authority in the classroom. As we shape a teaching self, we are in almost continual conversation with the internalized voices of people from our past: former teachers, teachers represented in popular culture and literature, family members, and peers. But this conversation is often unconscious and terribly messy. In the midst of this internal conversation, we may criticize ourselves for the profound disparity between what we imagine to be required of us in this role and what we are actually doing.

Like many new instructors confronting the problem of who to be in the writing classroom, I tried to imitate the good teachers I had had in the past. I imagined my first-year writing instructor, who would walk back and forth in the front of the classroom, reading a poem, cracking a joke, or telling a story about his granddaughter. He had seemed so at ease and confident in his directing of the class. I thought of other teachers as well, teachers who made me want to go home and write or stay up all night reading poetry. These teachers lived their subjects; they radiated excitement about the material and the students, and they never seemed afraid. But images of my former teachers did little to help me figure out how to conduct myself as a teacher in my classroom, to work productively with *my* 101 students. In fact, they underlined my self-doubt.

The problem with imagining myself as a teacher like my previous, almost-heroic instructors went beyond the fact that we were different people, teaching in different decades, with different students. Trying to be one of my former instructors, or some combination of them, meant somehow abandoning parts of myself. In my new role as teacher, I felt that I had to leave myself at the door, inject my former teachers' sensibilities into me, and go into class. I knew I couldn't do this. But I also knew that whoever I was in the classroom was not quite right yet, that the subjectivity of Dawn as teacher felt incommensurate to the job. I had heard that teachers become more comfortable with students over time, but I had no time to spare. I was losing my class.

In this chapter I examine how a new writing instructor negotiates the conflict between what a teacher should be and what we might call a "teaching self." Rather than providing a generic recipe for inventing a teaching self, I explore specific situations in which new instructors struggle to play the role of writing teacher as they connect with, feel disconnected from, and attempt to reconnect with students over and over again. I argue that important clues to fashioning a teaching self can be found in teachers' emotional responses to students and in what they can discern about students' emotional responses to them, particularly at the most difficult moments. The next step, I would suggest, is to try to identify, embrace, and make explicit use of our feelings, so that we can be more fully present to our students and invite them into more genuine interactions with us.

What I experienced in the classroom with my students on the third day of teaching evoked some of my most unwelcome feelings: fear, shame, and anger. Studies of new instructors invariably find that they express similar fears: of showing themselves as powerless, out of control, or unable to maintain their professional authority, fears that they do not really know who they are supposed to be in the classroom (Rankin). Jane Tompkins argues that one reason new teachers experience so much fear is that the model of teaching they are accustomed to is very much based on hierarchical models of achievement and performance: "Fear is the driving force behind the performance model. Fear of being shown up for what you are: a fraud, stupid, igno-

rant, a clod, a dolt, a sap, a weakling, someone who can't cut the mus-
tard. In graduate school especially, fear is prevalent. Thinking about
these things, I became aware recently that my own fear of being shown
up for what I really am must transmit itself to my students, and insofar
as I was afraid to be exposed, they too would be afraid" (17). Tompkins
suggests that teachers' fears can create or increase students' anxieties
and that teachers who are in graduate school are especially vulnerable,
by virtue of their institutional positions. Rankin's study would support
Tompkins's claim, for all the teachers she studied expressed anxieties
about being judged.

Tompkins and Rankin might easily be describing Lucy (all names
are pseudonyms), a beginning teacher at Emerson College. After her
second class, she was euphoric. "It was great," she said. "They were all
talking, and the text seemed to be opening up all over the place." But
after her third class she was devastated. She said it was as if they had
discussed it all previously and had only one thing to say about the text,
which was what they had already said in the previous class. It was like
those high school essays with a thesis statement plus three paragraphs,
she said, the ones in which students solve the problems of the world in
three steps and then remind us of what they've done.

There were other difficulties. She wrote me an e-mail about them
later. "It's as if I can't really be myself with them," she wrote:

> I know that students like a strict teacher, but I am not really a strict
> person. I don't like imposing on anybody. I don't like to think of myself
> as an authority or expert in the classroom. I am not. I know I'm not,
> and I don't know how to pretend like I am. What's more, I do not want
> to pretend. I see what a teaching persona is with my sister, and frankly,
> I think it's false and unnecessary. But then how do I be myself as the
> teacher? I don't care if they like me; they don't need to like me. I don't
> need to be their friend. I think I'm just a lot more easygoing than they
> need me to be. I'm not sure what I need to do or say in order to seem
> less easygoing without feeling like a phony. Tomorrow is only the
> fourth class, but I feel that if I don't cement the policies now, or at least
> understandings, then I won't be able to later on. So how do I do it?
> What do I say?

Lucy's message reverberates with uncertainty and questions. Who should she be? Who do they want her to be? I suggested to Lucy that, like teachers, students bring their most difficult feelings into the classroom, especially fear. Suddenly, as we began to discuss what her students might be afraid of, she seemed less frightened about her class having ground to a halt. I reminded her of her observations about the essay and suggested that she address students' fears about the difficulties of writing their first college essay. Their essays were not to follow the template that many of them were accustomed to using in high school, and no formula existed for what they were to be. She might remind them that writing is really hard work and makes her anxious—ready to clean the bathroom, raid the refrigerator, or call a friend.

Just as I could not think of how to act in front of my silenced students, Lucy could not offer her students a story of her own struggles because she was paralyzed by fear. And she could not retreat to the safety of what she knew because she had so little experience as a teacher. Her course in the theories and practices of teaching had given her no method for figuring out how to regain a firm footing in a moment of utter chaos in the classroom. In particular, she had no clue about how to calm the internal storm that this moment caused so that she could handle the external challenge.

Over the years, I have discovered the value of paying careful attention to what I am calling the "inner storm" that new instructors experience in their attempts to use authority productively in the classroom. This storm is an internal response to a mixture of things, including our institutional positions and the social categories that we are subject to both inside and outside the class: race, class, gender, ethnicity, sexuality, and religion, for example, but there are many more. Most personally, perhaps, the storm responds to students' interactions with us in the here and now.

Lucy's attention to her own inner storm relates to the concepts of self- and interactive regulation from infant research (Beebe and Lachmann 224). She actively compares what she is observing in herself to what she believes is happening in her students' minds. This process of checking in, which is very subtle, verifies whether Lucy is correct in assuming that students are bored or restless or confused. Lucy is learning to compare these observations with what she is feeling inside, to gauge where to take the group next or how to respond to a particular question or challenge.

The inner storm that Lucy experiences also harkens back to what we might call the "there and then," interactions from the past that somehow get rekindled in difficult moments (Herzog 31). Often, these interactions relate to times when we learned something about how people behave in positions of authority while we played the role of the less powerful figure in relation to that person. We might call these people, real and symbolic, the "ghosts of authority" in our classrooms. Lucy's ghosts include her sister, who is older and also a teacher and who has, in Lucy's words, bullied her since she was a small child. Lucy was afraid of becoming her sister in the classroom. But her ghosts also included people who know more than she about all kinds of things, especially teaching. They included men who had also asserted authority over her, as well as people who had criticized her for her religious devotion. Sorting out the threads of her strong reactions, those based in the here and now and those which reflect the there and then, offered one way for Lucy to identify her implicit ways of being in the classroom: of interacting with students, creating space for them or closing it down. She inherited these ways of being from the ghosts in her past and from the more general social institutions that haunt us all. Identifying these ghosts would make it easier for her to teach without being overwhelmed by their presence.

When Lucy and I next spoke, we discussed her fear from a different perspective. She said again, "I don't want to be like my sister." I asked her to tell me what that would look like. Lucy elaborated: "Well, I would be bossy and controlling. I would tell them what to do, how to do it, when to do it, and when to hand it in. I would not let them be themselves but would insist that they conform to my ideas about who they should be. I would talk a lot and listen not at all." I agreed with Lucy that this persona did not sound like a very good one for a teacher. And yet, the setting of boundaries was a necessary part of the job. I deliberated about how to proceed.

"I wonder if there is anything that is useful in what you just described," I mused. "Although I have to admit your sister sounds awful, I wonder if it might be bad for a teacher to be a bully, but also not great to be a pushover?"

Lucy nodded, commenting, "I do think I am a bit of a pushover right now."

"And I have been a bully," I said. "Like in the days when I taught at an urban middle school, and I didn't know how to keep the kids calm, so I made them each stand on a square of the classroom floor when they entered the room until they were quiet."

"Yuck," said Lucy. I nodded. We laughed.

"Well," Lucy thought out loud, "I think I might need to be a little more like a bully and a little less like a pushover. Maybe I need to set the same boundaries that my sister might, but in a different way, like the way my college writing instructor used to. He would tell us that it was our responsibility to ourselves, to him, and to the class to be on time, to have our work done, and to be ready to participate in our discussion. He was really calm, but he didn't take any crap." She also mentioned an English teacher in high school who said "you are taking advantage of my goodwill" when students started coming to class late. As a result, she allowed no students in the door if they appeared even five minutes after the class was to begin. "But nobody was late, either," said Lucy.

We discussed how "not taking any crap" could be very different from giving students crap just because we are the ones who hand out the grades, how it could be a way of setting the boundaries within which students work. When Lucy left my office, she had a more commanding gait; she seemed ready to take charge of her class. Her sense of what it meant to be a good teacher had been challenged, or disrupted, and had now been transformed into something else. And the class, as she told me later, was now prepared to meet the expectations she had for them. By the end of the term, her anxiety about holding power had become a challenge rather than an obstacle, something she thought about how to handle rather than fought as the enemy.

Deborah Britzman uses the term "personal practical knowledge" to explain that "knowledge made from the stuff of lived experience is so intimately a part of teachers' enactments that its appearance as skills becomes taken for granted. Taken for granted as well are how their discursive practices come to express something about the structure of institutional life, and the ways in which power and authority are experienced there" (*Practice Makes Practice* 4–5). Britzman describes the intersection of the personal and the institutional stories that inform our responses to students from moment to moment in the classroom. Lucy's "enactments" reflect her own "personal practical knowledge." They informed her internalized understanding of power and authority that was learned from her own familial and educational experiences, and her application of that understanding in interactions with her class. Once she became aware of not one but several internalized personae who were exerting authority within her, she seemed more willing to negotiate between them as she fashioned her own teaching self. Rather than simply resisting the strongest internalized authority figure of her sister, in a battle of two, Lucy had entered a conversation of many about how to hold power in a group.

Students are always accommodating to the interpersonal reality of the teacher's character and institutional positioning, and their accommodations, invisible to us, both reflect back to us our ways of teaching and help us to perpetuate them. This was the experience of Simon, an instructor who came to my office during the fourth week of the semester with an anxious expression on his usually serene face. "What am I going to do about Valerie?" he asked. Valerie? I repeated her name to try to get the situation back into my head. "Well, in class today, she offered another one of her zingers. She said that she didn't see the point of responding to a stupid question about some obscure readings that were arbitrarily chosen by her instructor." "And what did you say?" I asked. "Well, nothing really," he replied. "That's why I am here."

At Emerson College, undergraduates seem to feel particularly free to make comments like Valerie's. But these students will not be unfamiliar to teachers anywhere. They question their instructors about why they are writing the papers, why they are reading these readings, and why they have to take the course at all. They constitute a minority in that usually only one student per class tends to ask such questions, but a majority in the sense that every teacher has one. And for every teacher, these students seem to provoke intense anxiety about the teacher's authority and how to use it.

Students like Valerie present an extreme position, but they will be familiar to instructors who think carefully about how to assert authority in classrooms. In a classroom in which the teacher holds the answers to the student's every question, Valerie's challenge to the teacher's authority might be met by an answer like, "Because you are learning something about what it means to learn to write, which is something that I know about and you do not." But in what Paulo Freire terms a problem-posing classroom, the kind of classroom Simon said he was trying to create, "the teacher is no longer the one who teaches, but one who is himself taught in dialogue with the students, who in turn while being taught also teach" (67). In this kind of classroom, students and teachers together create what we call a "class." Student challenges might be heard as comments on what is happening in the classroom already, between the people in that room, rather than as simple affronts to the authority of the instructor.

Valerie's challenge provoked Simon to figure how to hold authority in a way that was both real and purposeful in the classroom. He needed to talk about reading and writing at the same time that he actually engaged his students as human beings. Simon needed to find ways to bring his whole self to the process of teaching if he was to engage his students' whole selves. He also needed to realize that his students, including Valerie, were struggling with their own demons. Like their teachers, they can sometimes feel overwhelmed and powerless, and therefore they too shut down.

Or they erupt. When Simon talked about Valerie, I had an image of an erupting volcano. I did not share this with him, in part because I wasn't sure who was the volcano: Simon, Valerie, or the pair. I also wondered if I could be the volcano, given my concern that the class was slipping away from Simon. Keeping these thoughts to myself, I asked him what was going through *his* head as Valerie spoke.

"I was terrified," he said. "I figured there was no way I could justify myself. I mean, I've only been teaching for four weeks. What do I know?" I wondered to myself if Valerie had an inkling that this was how Simon felt; perhaps she had launched the question to articulate just that.

But I also wondered if Valerie had made Simon angry. I wondered this because of the volcano image in my head, but also because it seemed so likely. Angry students provoke our anger. I told Simon that I had had students like Valerie myself and that they made me angry, because they were questioning everything about the course, and not just what was happening at the moment. They took me away from what I was trying to accomplish with students and focused me on global issues that were not foremost in my mind. They also questioned my presence in the room as the teacher, and I already questioned that about myself. And I told him that I did not need a student to amplify my self-doubt.

But what to do, I asked aloud? I placed the question between us. I wondered what a really good teacher would do at that moment, underlining the fact that this would be our fantasy about both of us as the failed instructors trying to find our way. Simon and I began to talk about what it means to be a really good teacher, and to him, it meant being a person who *knows* something he can share with others. He described a teacher in his undergraduate institution who knew all about southern literature. Implicit in his description was a theory of knowledge as expert, factual, and book driven, as well as embodied in a person who is older, with a Ph.D. Simon knew that he should have something to say about writing, because he was the teacher, but he also knew that he could not be the teacher because he did not fit with the image—we might say, the ghost—of a knowledgeable person in a classroom that he had imagined. As he spoke, I was imagining a man with a beard and a tweed jacket: a contrast to the slim figure in khakis and a button-down shirt in front of me. I was struck by how the image in Simon's mind was much less interesting to me than Simon himself. He was a witty, playful, and creative conversationalist. He was also very mature and offered insights to other teachers in our meetings. He was reflective and calm.

I decided that we should discuss something in which Simon did feel like an expert, because it might restore his sense of safety before we continued. I asked him what he knew about his own writing process. He began to talk about discipline and difficulty, about how writing takes time, about the importance of reading to learn about style and to expand one's consciousness. These seemed to me to be very important ideas to present to a writing class, I offered. I noticed that Simon seemed different as he talked about this. He seemed to sit up straighter in his chair, to become thoughtful, probing, and relaxed. I wondered aloud if it might be useful for him to share with his students these aspects of what it means to learn to write, and he said that he hadn't really considered it. He seemed relieved to have found something he might say to Valerie and her classmates. What he had found was almost a cliché to him, knowledge close to his understanding of what it means to write, even to be alive.

I believe that Simon did not consider talking about his sense of what it means to be a writer because assuming the role of teacher can prompt us to lose sight of ourselves as struggling human beings who have limited power in the world and make us feel that we need to sound like people who know what we are doing. As part of this, we leave behind our student selves and try to sound like teaching selves. But there are students in the room with us, and we need to find ways to connect with them as individuals and as a group. To this day, this aspect of teaching remains implicit, almost magical, and is rarely discussed in our literature in any detail. And no matter how many techniques we hear about from our colleagues and from teaching manuals, it is not a static process. *In First Day to Final Grade: A Graduate Student's Guide to Teaching,* Anne Curzan and Lisa Damour point out the conflict between playing a role and feeling authentic: "New teachers often need to rely on 'the rules' (guidelines, due dates, syllabi) and on established teacher-student roles to create a feeling of authority. For example, many teaching assistants start by imitating favorite teachers of their own. As you get more experience and confidence, you will be able to act more natural in your role as an instructor. You will then be able to be more yourself while being a teacher"

(121). Although patience and time present crucial factors in teacher development, I think that ways exist to help a new teacher be herself and act naturally other than simply waiting for the feeling to take hold. What is "natural" for a new teacher, in other words, is not teaching. But even time and doing it will not necessarily make teaching come naturally to us. We all know plenty of teachers who do not seem comfortable in the classroom after years of teaching.

For Parker Palmer, a teacher's self-knowledge is essential to this sense of confidence. In *The Courage to Teach*, Palmer argues that a teacher who learns to pay careful attention to her or his inner life produces a classroom presence that feels real to students. Wondering "who is the self that teaches?" Palmer notes that "technique" is what teachers employ until the real teacher arrives (7). He contends that we need to reclaim ourselves for the sake of our students. Stephen Brookfield, in *The Skillful Teacher*, underlines the value of developing an "inner voice": "Until you begin to trust your inner voice, until you accept the possibility that your instincts, intuitions, and insights often possess as much validity as those of the experts in the field, and until you recognize that in the contexts in which you work *you* are the expert, there is a real danger that a profoundly debilitating sense of inadequacy may settle on you" (14). Brookfield and Palmer are echoed by many theorists who underline the emotional state of the instructor as essential to teaching success.

In their emphasis on the teacher's inner life, however, these theorists do not entirely take into account the dynamic and constantly-in-flux relationships between teachers and those in their environment. These relationships call on and alter a teacher's inner life in innumerable ways. Moreover, they call into question the usefulness of speaking about the teacher's inner life without simultaneously addressing the life of the classroom—daily interactions with students. Britzman advises that "the unitary, noncontradictory humanist discourse of the completed self" of a teacher should be replaced by "a provisional, contradictory, and multiple understanding of subjectivity as both individual and social" (*Practice Makes Practice* 56–57). Britzman's postmodern definition of the self complicates linear understandings of a teacher's development as a confident and authoritative presence in the classroom. Maxine Greene offers a similar discussion of the teacher's self: "One's 'reality,' rather than being fixed and predefined, is a perpetual emergent, becoming increasingly multiplex, as more perspectives are taken, more texts are opened, more friendships are made" (23).

I am particularly interested in Greene's use of the term "emergent," because it represents the teacher interacting in his or her environment in an ongoing way and being shaped by those interactions. Simon does this as he becomes more curious about what his students are evoking in him and more uncertain about where they might be heading together. At the same time, he needs to be able to articulate what he, the instructor, is trying to accomplish with this particular group of students. These two aims, open-ended curiosity and certainty about the goals of the group, are indeed at cross-purposes. Still, somehow they must work together. It is as if we need to go into ourselves and out again; a successful relationship with ourselves as teachers and with a particular group of students involves negotiation and conflict as well as tremendous self-awareness. And it requires a very close attention to what can often seem like business as usual.

The concept of "emergence" is also central to nonlinear dynamic systems theory, a theory to which I have turned in my efforts to conceptualize how the interactions between a teacher and her students facilitate the development of what I term a "teaching self." Nonlinear dynamic systems theory, which originated from principles developed in physics, chemistry, and mathematics, "concern[s] problems of emergent order and complexity: how structure and patterns arise from the cooperation of many individual parts" (Thelen and Smith xiv). Nonlinear systems theory offers a view of how systems develop over time that is based on unpredictability. In dynamic systems theory, the self consists of two conflicting impulses: one, "the sense and experience of cohesiveness and continuity across time," and two, "the experience . . . of self states which can be described as multiple, shifting, nonlinear, and discontinuous" (Beebe and Lachmann 232). In other words, the developing self seeks coherence and continuity even as it is in motion, changing over time. The constant flux in our classrooms is obvious to us, and yet its implications for the teaching self, particularly the motion back and forth from what is stable to what is not, are less obvious.

First, classroom interactions take place in what we might call the "split-second world," a term coined by infant researcher Daniel Stern that describes how babies respond to their mothers as active agents, from moment to moment, almost from birth (*Interpersonal World of the Infant* 10). Although Stern uses the term to capture interactions between mother and infant and trace the infant's participation in the process of making meaning, it is useful as a way to understand any human interaction. Stern and other infant researchers make use of dynamic systems theory as they attempt to understand how infants and mothers transform from moment to moment in their interactions. In the classroom, interactions happen in a group rather than a dyad, and they are terribly subjective and fast-paced, especially for the new teacher.

Second, our capacity for organizing ourselves in front of a class is at its most precarious when we first begin to teach. In fact, in nonlinear systems theory "the transformation from the old state to the new state takes place when the system is maximally vibrating and in its least predictable condition" (Stechler 77). The new teacher might be considered, in this sense, a maximally vibrating system, as might the class of students he is trying to work with, and the inner storm that Simon described would be an indicator of the internal ramifications for the new teacher. Systems theory suggests that the "local system" may be "maximally influencing the environment" at a moment of transformation. Thus, our students provide maximal influences in our first year as a teacher, which means that dealing with them in productive ways is essential to our development as instructors. It also means that our earliest students have an influence on us that our later students will find in their classrooms. We can trust students' responses, in other words, to show us some way of becoming ourselves in the classroom.

The idea that Valerie could be helpful to Simon was exactly the opposite of what Simon thought was happening, and yet I asked him to consider it as an enabling fiction in order to facilitate the repair that I believed the two needed to achieve. But first I urged Simon to get in touch with his rage at Valerie. I asked him if he was not trusting his reactions to her because he felt that they were inappropriate: that a good teacher should never be angry at a student, and perhaps even that an older male teacher should not be angry at a female student. But being angry and acting angrily, I told him, are different. If he could trust his anger, he might find a way to make use of it and then to make a decision about what he wanted to have happen. He could, for example, use his anger to gain intensity in the classroom. He could also use his anger to make a connection with his angry student. He could embrace his anger by jumping into the room with both feet, taking hold of Valerie's question, and turning it into an issue for the class rather than a problem between him and his student. In other words, he might find a new way to connect with his student and his entire class as a result of a frightening interaction with one student.

Whatever he decided, I was trying to help Simon make use of what he was feeling rather than abandoning himself as a teacher and retreating to a position of the failed teacher who is waiting for the expert to arrive. I was crafting a theory of expertise with Simon that related to paying close attention to his feelings and responses to students in a single moment and then making explicit use of them. Simon's internal storm of anger and frustration signaled his unconscious participation in a maximally vibrating classroom system, a system ripe for change, on the brink of chaos. By attending to the part that he played in that system and by thinking carefully about the components of his own internal storm, he could ideally find a way to connect with his students and bring them all into a new understanding of what they were trying to achieve together.

One of the primary ways in which I found my own response to Simon was through the volcano image, which I took to reflect the storminess of his internal world as a teacher, the storminess of his student's internal world, and the storm of my own response to the teacher's distress. I was a maximally vibrating administrator who worried that the writing program was without a purpose. Searching for a story from my experience to calm myself, I recalled a moment from the earliest days of my teaching career, when another teacher told me how she handled a crush she had developed on a student. At first she was mortified, imagining they knew that she was not qualified to teach, that she was immature and lascivious, the female version of the lecherous male professor. Once she calmed down and realized that she would never act on her response to the student, she decided to try to find a different use for her feelings. Rather than banishing them from the room, she decided to bring her loving feelings to the entire class—in her words, to have a love affair with her class. The teacher said that she decided to pay more attention to the way she looked, to dress up for her class, as a way to let them know that they mattered to her. She prepared very carefully, with these particular students in mind. Her crush on one student turned into a new interest in teaching. In other words, her idea worked. Her desire for them seemed to feed theirs for the material they were working on together.

This teacher's ability to transform a potential disaster into a productive classroom has been of use to me in numerous interactions with teachers who are developing their teaching selves. My former colleague's example of energy being freed up and fired up has been helpful to keep in mind. It is also useful to think that students, like their teachers, want to be authentic participants in the educational process. And like their teachers, they fail at this all the time. A teacher who is herself in the classroom offers the gift of authenticity to her students. Students know when we are faking it, and they know when we are not owning our role in the story. They know, for example, when we are expressing enthusiasm for a comment or a paper that we do not actually love all that much. Students want honesty, although they may resist it, and they want permission to be themselves. Like their teachers, they know what they can voice in a certain situation and what the consequences are. Seen in this way, teaching is not like building a model airplane, getting the right part in the right order. It is dealing with real people rather than the roles to which they are assigned, and reaching inside to figure out what feels right about that.

Matthew, a confident, brilliant man and an already published writer, came to see me in despair after his second week of teaching. He felt that his students were walking all over him. They were so lively in the discussions that they almost shouted over each other to speak. One student insisted on having conversations with the people next to him throughout the class; others waltzed in fifteen minutes late. Matthew's warnings about the late policy seemed to be ignored, as did the discussions he held about listening carefully to each other and waiting for one's turn to speak. I knew Matthew to be a very successful horse trainer, and I asked what he did with unruly horses. "Oh, I know how to handle them," he said. "But these are people, and there are many of them, not just one. I am sure they know that I am new at this, and they are taking full advantage."

I offered to visit Matthew's classroom, to see the group for myself, and to offer the students a quick introduction to the college writing program, which I do every year in every class. When I arrived, the students and the instructor were in a heated discussion of a Susan Bordo essay about the female body. Each student had an advertisement on his or her desk. Questions about Bordo's theories and their relationship to the advertisements covered the board. The atmosphere was lively and engaging. But it did seem as if some of the students were talking at the same time, and one student appeared to be conducting his own class in the corner of the circle. Matthew was in the front of the room, but he seemed nervous. His arms hugged his chest, and his body was turned slightly away from his students. It was almost as if he were trying to hide in plain sight.

After Matthew introduced me, I spoke to the students about the program, detailing the requirements, the sequence of writing courses, and the portfolio grading specifications. As I spoke, the lively student in the corner spoke to his neighbor. I noticed that I was feeling irritated with him and nervous that he was attempting to derail the class. I decided to be polite, because I was feeling that he was most impolite. "Oh, I'm sorry," I said. "I didn't know you wanted to speak."

"No, it was nothing," he said, smiling at me and at the students around him.

"Oh, okay." I said. "Now back to the portfolio."

After a couple of minutes he had begun to talk to his neighbors again. This time I found myself feeling less anxious, more ready to handle the situation. I looked him in the eye with an expression that might be described as quizzical and asked him if he had wanted to say something. When he said no, I said, "I'm sorry, I just got confused. It looked as if you had something you wanted to ask or say." He said no, and smiled again. I smiled. I was having fun with him, and everyone knew it. But he was having some fun too, I gathered, and no harm had yet been done.

When this sequence was repeated for a third time, I tried a different tactic. After asking him if he wanted to speak, and being told no, I laughed, and said, "You'll have to forgive me. I am getting so old that I can't speak and listen at the same time." I was making fun of myself, exaggerating my weaknesses even as I made it clear that I was older and very much in charge. I was also clarifying what was happening—the student was talking over me. Everyone laughed, including Matthew.

But I was worrying that this student was hinting at some discontent in the class as a whole. I decided to play around with this by posing and answering some devil's advocate questions of my own design. I raised questions to the class, saying: "Let's play devil's advocate. What if this portfolio is a waste of time? Why write so many essays?" A number of students hypothesized that I could be correct; they were, after all, seasoned writers. What did they need to learn? I said that they were unlike me at their age, because I had lacked confidence in myself as a writer. In fact, I noted, I still had trouble writing. I struggled to figure out what it was I was trying to say, and I asked my peers to help me define and refine my arguments. A couple of students raised their hands to say that they were more like me. They struggled with writing and worried that they were not ready to write college essays. Several others nodded. I said that perhaps there were some lessons to be learned in 101, but that if they had doubts, they were always welcome to take up their concerns with their teacher and with me. Let's give it a little time, I said, and then see where you are.

My conversation with the students is difficult to characterize, because it is so firmly based in the particulars of these students, their teacher, and me. I would not have made some of the statements I did in the way that I did in a different classroom. I developed a sense of where these students were, and I went with it. It is also very much based on eye contact and the way we held our bodies, the space we occupied, and the movements we made as we spoke and listened. When they laughed and seemed to be enjoying themselves, for example, I kept going in the direction I was heading in, because it looked like it was working. When they grew quiet, I withdrew a bit to assess the situation. But even as I responded to this group, I drew from what I knew about students' doubts concerning composition courses over the years. I pursued students' uncertainties, which I might at one time have determined as stemming from my own inadequacies as a teacher. In a way, I attempted to make use of John Keats's concept of "negative capability," which I had learned about when I was their age: "That is when man is capable of being in uncertainties, mysteries, doubt, without any irritable reaching after fact and reason" (Keats 43). What I once might have tried to hide, I now shaped into material for the class to discuss.

It is important to identify how the unruly student played a part in this dynamic and how I found a way to work with him and his classmates despite the irritation that he provoked. At first, his comments distracted me, and I looked over at him, wanting him to stop so that I could continue speaking. As he ignored my gaze and continued to speak, I became more irritated. He seemed to become louder, although this may have been my imagination. The longer he spoke and the more he tried to speak (this must in reality have been a matter of minutes), the more distracted and irritated I became. I was aware that I was beginning to feel angry and that I wanted to tell him to be quiet, that he was rude. I knew that this would not work, however. First, I was a visitor in his class; second, if I were to attack him this way, both he and his classmates would lose respect for me.

I then tried to make use of my anger by transforming it into something different: curiosity. When that did not work, and my anger increased, I tried another option: playful but subdued banter. Finally,

I moved to more pronounced banter. With each step, I checked the reactions of the class and the student as I proceeded. If they had seemed provoked or angered or insulted, I might have backed off and waited a bit before pursuing the difficulty. If it were my own class, I would have considered a pedagogical tool such as the one-minute essay or a quick, directed group exercise to change the energy in the room. Changing the energy in the room was directly related, of course, to changing the energy in myself—from anger to something more useful. The energy in myself might also be termed "counter-transference," which I discuss in chapter 3.

This movement from the inside to the outside is essential to the work of a successful teacher who is authoritative and authentic in the classroom, and expert teachers make such a move unconsciously. When we slow down the process, as I did above, we can see that there is a constant shifting from recognizing our own feelings to attempting to perceive the feelings of our students, to using our feelings as we respond to what we believe is happening with our students. All of this occurs in the background as we are talking about something quite different: the reading for the day, an aspect of writing, a sample paper, or a grammatical issue. In the example above, I tried to respond without anger, fear, or self-doubt; these are unproductive emotions for an authority figure to voice toward students most of the time, but they are certainly useful when transformed into something else.

We might imagine that the balance between our internal experiences and our external actions involves a balance between self and other. But psychoanalytic theory and infant research provide another way of understanding this movement: "What is in balance is not self and other, but, rather, the processes of self- and interactive regulation. Each person is always sensing and modulating her own state, while simultaneously sensing how she affects and is affected by her partner. What is in balance is the degree to which one can flexibly go back and forth, in foreground-background fashion, between both processes" (Beebe and Lachmann 244). Improvisational theater offers the same point from a different perspective: "Practice in improvisational theatre . . . enhance[s] the teacher's ability to be 'in the moment,' to be flexible, to temporarily suspend their teaching strategies or their rules about their relationship with their student in order to enter into an authentic, personal interaction" (Tiberius and Tipping 11).

My effort to be authentic with the student concluded when he came up after class to chat a bit about the course. His first words were that he was dyslexic. He said that he had never done well in a writing class before, and he was sure he wouldn't this time. His teacher, he, and I discussed the Learning Assistance Center. He agreed that he would go there and that he would visit my office to discuss what, if anything, the Composition Program could do to help him. It seemed to me that, as is often the case, this student disrupted the class because of his own self-doubts. He was afraid he did not belong in this class, that he could not do the work required. He spoke to his classmate while I was speaking as a way of participating in the class by exerting some control, perhaps, or to distract himself from the enormous anxieties provoked by his presence there.

The teacher came to visit me after the class and looked enormously relieved. "That was weird," he said. "Watching you in class, I remembered having you as a teacher. It felt like you were just being yourself with them, and they responded to that. At the same time, they got that you meant business. I think I have been struggling with how to be myself and also mean business, and I thought that it was impossible to do both at the same time."

The question is how a teacher becomes confident in his work, a teacher who "means business," even as he "is himself" in the classroom. In the story above, that involved trying to figure out where the students were while keeping sight of where the teacher wanted them to be. The difficult student in the corner, I had mused, wanted attention, but he also wanted to invent a new class over in the corner to substitute for the one I was leading. I wanted us to be one class, working on the problem of writing successful research papers together, and so I had to harness the student's energy and move it in a different direction. But whether we moved in such a direction depended very much on the student's willingness to go there. In our dialogue, I implicitly asked his permission to join me in this new venture.

My friend Barrie, a teacher whom I have known for almost twenty years, recently showed me her first teaching notebook. It contained page after page of color-coded charts. Some of the charts denoted sample quotations from the text; others, possible questions; and others, possible answers. If a student answered A on question 1 about line 3 of the poem, then she'd proceed to the orange question 2, which went deeper into that line. But if the student answered B, then she'd try question 4, which headed to another part of the poem. And so on. We laughed and laughed as we looked at this notebook, imagining ourselves trying to use such a complex script now, so many years after we had begun teaching. And yet, my friend said rather seriously, she would have felt completely lost without it then.

Barrie's system, bizarre as it may sound, gave her a feeling of control over the direction of the class. But unlike a lecture, it had options. So she felt that she could give her students room to explore many directions rather than simply one. Students could produce many interpretations of a poem, for example, and many essays about it. Now, she does not need the chart because she has learned how to be open to students' ideas in a classroom without losing sight of a direction in which the class can move.

Becoming yourself as a teacher involves, more than anything, telling yourself who you are and who you are not in the classroom. Although we might have trouble remembering who we are not at the most difficult times, we are not the fearful daughters, sons, and students that we once might have been. We are not the students who, like my friend Marie, had a famous professor in graduate school who wrote on her evaluation, "Very poorly trained when she got here, she gets nearly everything wrong. She should not be allowed to remain in a graduate program in English." Yet we sometimes react as if we were still in these roles. We defensively make statements as I did in my first week of teaching: "It's not my job to keep the discussion going."

When we become ourselves in the writing classroom, we offer students opportunities rather than accusations. We channel our fears into productive comments. During a silence, we might ask them to find a quote and share it with the class. Or when a student seems to need attention, we might direct attention to the context of the classroom, for example, or use the needy student as a volunteer for a writing workshop. We work with our students and attempt to clear a space for everyone to speak. We call on students to invite them into the conversation and work to link one student's comments to another's.

In addition to all this, the teacher acts as the living memory for the class. We hold the class up to the class in front of our students, to show them who we are and what we are making together. We remind the class of where we have been together and where we are heading. In this way, we bring the outside world into the classroom to be transformed into knowledge. We remind our students that we are thinking about them when we are not in the classroom, that conversations we've had in class have influenced our understanding of events that have happened outside class. In the process, we initiate our students into an intellectual world in which school and the outside are part of the same continuum, a world in which reading and writing are real and in which real change can happen from the knowledge that we construct together.

Most of us would admit that fear poses a challenge in our lives. But can we move beyond fear, or embrace our fear, in order to create beauty in the classroom? When the classroom becomes a place where students can feel their fear, and any other feeling that they experience as forbidden, they no longer need to separate the process of learning from the process of being human. And when teachers do the same, however silently, we join students in the effort to achieve deeper understanding. Teaching and learning involve being in the moment in a total way, as a whole person. When there is a disruption, such as those I described above, a teacher can embrace the experience rather than trying to send it out of the room. If we accept fear as part of who we are, we can be fully present in the moment and open to the experience of a changing classroom that is part of a changing world.

CHAPTER TWO

THE FREEZE FRAME
Ways of Reading Classroom Discussion

> We talk with one another only on those occasions
> where what we are talking about hovers ahead of us
> and gradually takes shape for all of us—where we in
> effect discover only at the end of the discussion the
> topic which got the discussion started.
>
> —Cyril Welch, "Talking"

"THEY WOULDN'T ANSWER MY QUESTION." "THEY LOOKED AT ME as if I had just spoken another language." "I don't think they read the assigned text." "It was like pulling teeth." We have all taught classes in which the discussion simply does not work. When we try to describe what happens in these hours, we often use visceral images that depict us as dentists pulling teeth from patients who have not been given anesthetic, or miracle workers, raising bodies from the dead. We cast ourselves as hardworking professionals who face crowds of lazy, passive, or baffled students.

When the discussion is not working, we invoke our authority and expertise as teachers to investigate the problem of what to do. But when our discussions go well, we are more likely to use plural pronouns and emotive imagery to talk about them. We say that "we were in the groove," "on the same wavelength," or "tuned in." When it goes well, in other words, we relax into it; we let it flow. We become an earnest group of human beings thinking and arguing together. But what are we doing when the discussion is at its best? How does a teacher use his or her expertise to transform a mass of individuals into a community of thinkers on any given day? In short, what does a teacher do to make the discussion come alive?

In excellent teaching manuals such as Wilbert McKeachie's *Teaching Tips*, Stephen Brookfield and Stephen Preskill's *Discussion as a Way of Teaching*, and Katherine Gottschalk's *Facilitating Discussion*, we find recommendations about how to initiate and sustain student discussions. Gottschalk argues that discussions should have a clear beginning and end, for example, and that teachers need to practice waiting rather than jumping in to respond to their own questions. She suggests transforming students' statements into questions, writing on the board as the students talk, and putting students into groups so that they can generate questions and interpretations together (8–9).

Most of these suggestions, and those in other manuals as well, approach the leading of discussion from cognitive and procedural perspectives—what to do to generate a discussion, how to echo, incorporate, and build on students' ideas. These strategies can be very helpful to us if we think of ourselves as doctors, for example, honing the instruments of our discussion-leading technique: what to say, what to ask, how to build a structure of thought in a classroom. They all invoke an instructor who "operates" in the room, a professional who practices a particular technique or performs a set of functions—an instructor who might be needed to save situations that feel like "pulling teeth."

But even armed with these good ideas, we sometimes confront troubling silences and abysmal stalemates in our classrooms. We have difficulties despite what we know about how to lead a discussion, I believe, because important aspects of leading discussion cannot be accounted for by cognitive or procedural knowledge. Those of us who try to reach students in a class discussion know that there is a highly subjective level to what we do—a level beyond cognitive understanding. But how do we become conscious of the grammars of our interactions with students in the classroom? Drawing from my own experiences facilitating classroom discussions, from those of the teachers I supervise, and from recent literature in the fields of education, composition, psychoanalytic theory, and infant research, I attempt to answer this question in the pages that follow. I will examine moment-to-moment interactions between students and teachers in discussions that may seem just fine but are not, using them as sources of information about how to be more successful teachers of writing. When teachers monitor their own and their students' reactions in the here-and-now of a discussion, I argue, they can first identify and then make explicit use of their ways of interacting with students in the classroom as clues to improving their pedagogy.

To begin to think about what is happening (from the perspective of teaching) in a discussion that is moving along, I consider its opposite: the interpersonal dynamics of moments of disruption, moments when the discussion is not working. I also introduce a pedagogical tool, "the freeze frame," that I have found useful to my understanding of the classroom discussion. The freeze frame refers to a process through which we examine student-teacher interactions in a classroom by stopping the action to talk about what is happening at any given moment. The freeze frame is a break from the action, in which the facilitator halts the action of the discussion to draw our attention to what we are feeling in the room, what we are creating with the rest of the class, and how we are expanding ourselves as thinkers and writers. The majority of freeze frames are initiated because of the discussion leader's perception that something is not happening in the room that should be happening or because of her or his confusion about how to proceed. They also, more infrequently, occur at moments when the discussion is going well and the leader does not know why or how this happened.

The freeze frame, which can be used in any undergraduate or graduate classroom, offers students and teachers opportunities to think together about the local level of classroom discussions. At any moment in the discussion, in other words, an instructor might ask what is in the middle of our classroom space—what are we thinking about together now? Teachers can practice this way of listening to collect and make use of information about how they and their students separately and together contribute to class discussions in writing courses, one moment at a time.

Of course, mine is not the first attempt to identify forms of knowledge in the classroom that go beyond the cognitive level. Many of us have heard the call for alternative ways of knowing in the disciplines in more-recent years; in educational theory the call often appeals to relational and affective experiences as forms of knowledge. Deborah Tannen, for example, suggests that what she calls our "argument culture" tends to "value formal, objective knowledge over relational, intuitive knowledge" (255). Educational theorists beginning with Howard Gardner contribute to this discussion when they show us how to teach not one but "multiple intelligences." Daniel Goleman has discussed one of these forms of intelligence, which he calls "emotional intelligence," for almost two decades (43).

Goleman and others who explore emotions in the classroom tend to focus on how teachers might encourage students to think about themselves and others as people with feelings that are part of their understanding of what they learn. Megan Boler argues that feelings do not simply "appear" in classrooms; schools shape students' emotional worlds in attempts to produce "moral character" (32). Boler is joined by a chorus of writers who are concerned about how emotions function as sites of control in schooling (Cintron 595; Johnson, "School Sucks" 639).

Despite all this attention to feelings in the classroom, however, these writers focus primarily on students as the emotive, multi-intelligent beings to whom teachers direct their lessons. Their focus on students' emotional lives and how we shape them is both refreshing and long needed, but their tendency to invoke teachers as conveyors of skills and aptitudes, as observers of students' emotional lives, obfuscates the reality that teachers are emotive beings themselves, complex people who interact with individual students in numerous and shifting ways, from class to class, and even from moment to moment. These writers do not, in other words, focus directly on the importance of the interactions of students and teachers in the classroom. In building relationships with individual students and entire classes, we shape meanings—both separately and together—and always in ways that involve our emotional, intellectual, and physical lives.

Safety, comfort, and psychology directly relate to the learning our students do, but these concepts are often felt to be too abstract, personal, or variable for us to identify and to explain. I have been trying to develop a language to describe these aspects of teaching with graduate students in a course in composition theory and practice that I teach each semester. How does one speak about a teacher's "felt sense" of what it means to lead a classroom discussion? One of the major requirements of the graduate course is that students lead two class discussions of forty-five minutes each. My students and I developed the freeze frame in our efforts to find a language with which to explain the relationships that we were building and maintaining together in these discussions and the space in which to consider how these relationships influence the work we are doing. In a recent freeze frame, for example, the discussion leader stopped the action of the discussion because nobody was responding to her questions about the essay by Robert Coles that the class had read. She had asked, "What do you think is Coles's main point here?" and "How would you describe Coles's evidence?" The class was silent. Several students looked down and started looking at the text. Others simply stared in front of them.

The tension became palpable; the discussion leader's color rose. Her next comment was, "Freeze frame. Why is this happening?" Her classmates attributed their silence to the fact that they had just gotten into class and had not settled into a conversation yet. They hypothesized that soon they would find some question engaging enough to leave the places they'd been when they entered the room and join in the pursuit together of something important. We began to talk about the rhythm of a discussion, how it happens that a discussion takes off, and what that feels like to both student and teacher. We concluded that the teacher's questions needed to be more open at that moment, so that teachers and students could find a place to speak from which involved their experiences and the text they were investigating. We also thought that the questions needed to solicit specifically the students' experiences of reading the text for that day's class—what had they felt or thought when they read? The "solutions" these student teachers offered were practical and concrete, but the way that they found them was not. They arrived at them through a process of inquiry that began with a teacher's feeling of frustration and a group of students' equally frustrating (perhaps) feeling of not being invited to speak about something near to their experience.

Establishing, sustaining, and building the psychological climate of a college classroom is, to my mind, one of the most difficult and opaque aspects of teaching. The freeze frame provides a way for students and teachers to discuss this facet of pedagogy from the vantage point of their subjective experiences of the discussion at any given moment. In my continuing effort to find a language to describe what we are trying to talk about when we call a freeze frame, I have turned with excitement and great interest to scholarship on the production of knowledge in infant research. Infant researchers and psychoanalysts in the Boston Process of Change Study Group (the Boston Group) analyze interactions between mothers and babies and between patients and analysts in an attempt to distinguish between "two kinds of knowledge . . . one is explicit (declarative) and the other is implicit (procedural)" (Stern et al. 904). Explicit knowledge, or "knowing that," describes content matter. It is part of our conscious knowledge, which is rendered "in verbal or imagistic or symbolic form" (904). In a classroom, explicit knowledge might describe what we know about Robert Coles's essay, about how to construct thesis statements, or about a student's evidence-rich essay. Implicit knowledge, or "knowing how," is largely unconscious; it describes experiences that may elude our abilities to articulate how we do them. We may know how to ride a bike, for example, but can we say what exactly we know? (904). In a classroom, implicit knowledge would include teachers' and students' knowledge about human relationships, their sense of how to be with other people in a classroom. It might include, for example, how a teacher uses her voice to get students to quiet down or liven up, or how a student decides when he or she is welcome to enter a discussion.

Each of the words in the term "implicit relational knowledge" bears examination if we are to understand how the concept points to a neglected component of our pedagogical repertoire. "Implicit" suggests that this knowledge is not recognized or spoken about directly. It might refer, for example, to a teacher's sense of how to walk into a classroom for the first time and begin to teach a class. "Relational" implies that this form of knowledge is about relationships, about people coexisting and working together in particular ways. It might represent what a teacher meant when she told me how her class responded to her statement that they had to have their papers in her hands by ten o'clock in the morning on Wednesday. "Feel the love," one of them said; all the students laughed in response. The students' laughter implied that their teacher was not their all-accepting, touchy-feely mother figure at that moment—that, if anything, she was offering them tough love. That the student felt comfortable making this joke, and that the others felt safe enough to guffaw, suggests that this instructor had established an atmosphere of mutual respect and safety prior to this moment; they reflected it back when they emphasized her boundary setting as a part of their work together. This seemingly irrelevant joking is actually central to their work; it is a part of the implicit knowledge they are building together, one of their many ways of understanding "how to be" in their classroom. The word "knowledge" here refers to ways of knowing that we do not necessarily consider when we hear the word, because although the medium is linguistic, the moves we observe here and the patterns that emerge are not language based but address our felt sense of what it means to be individuals in relationship with others in our classroom.

Implicit relational knowledge includes how students and teachers interact in what infant researchers call the "split-second world" where experiences exist on "a phenomenological level, rather than a discussion of abstract meanings, although the phenomena are of course meaningful" (Stern, *Interpersonal World of the Infant* 4). These "phenomena" include how the student teacher above moved her body when she asked what Coles is talking about in his essay, or how the students shuffled their papers and feet or moved their eyes toward the ground in response. It concerns the devilish expression on the face of the student who said "feel the love," or his teacher's look of mock exasperation in response. The minutiae of this split-second world in a classroom are rarely, if ever, discussed in this detail, but it is certainly what we refer to when we say, for example, that the discussion "wouldn't move" or that it "felt like it was going in circles."

It might seem that attending to the implicit relational dimension of facilitating a discussion is tangential to the real work of discussion—the conceptual work—but implicit relational knowledge is not unrelated to content, to what we are trying to teach our students. Boston Group researcher Karlen Lyons-Ruth notes that implicit relational knowledge is "grounded in goal-directed action, along with the affective evaluations guiding that action, so *it is likely to exert as much or more influence on how symbolic systems are elaborated as symbolic systems exert on how relational systems are elaborated*" (2; emphasis added). Symbolic systems include our uses of language: the stories that we tell each other and ourselves concerning what we are thinking about together. Relational systems do not always include symbols; they refer to our interactions with each other, our ways of being with each other. Another way to say this is that what is going on between and among the people in the room bears an important relationship to what the students in the room actually learn. It lays the groundwork for that learning and ensures the circumstances under which it can continue.

Implicit relational knowledge might explain part of what a new teacher in the writing program I coordinate described in her experience leading class-room discussions: "When they leave and it's been a good discussion, I feel like the team has succeeded. I want to give them the high five. I really do feel pumped up. If it has not worked, I feel deflated. I keep thinking that if I analyze it I will figure out how to make it work. I am convinced that I did something wrong. I think about what I said or did not say, and what happened in the group, and I ask them what is working or not."

Two observations stand out in this description. The first is that the teacher describes the effect of a good discussion from the inside out. It is a feeling in her body; she feels "pumped up" when it works and "deflated" when it does not. A very important aspect of a teacher's implicit relational knowledge about the changing relationships between her and her students exists in her experience in her body, what she knows in her bones about what is or is not happening in her classroom. It is something she knows about from a feeling sense as much as from a cognitive impression. The second observation is that this teacher compares the discussion to a game that she and the students play: an "it"—a thing that is not the teacher or the individual students but what they are making and doing together. She does not explain the rules of their game because they are implicit. But she and her students know what is happening when she wants to give them "the high five." The implicit, largely nonverbal relationships in this teacher's classroom contribute to her students' sense of what it means to be in that room and to their sense of what they might create together in that space.

Donald Winnicott's concept of "potential space" that children and their mothers create when they are at play provides another way of understanding this aspect of classroom experience (*Maturational Process* 54). Extending his description of play as a universal event, Winnicott imagines the "potential space" that is not located in the child or in the mother but something they create together—much like the understanding of the teacher and her students of the possibilities in the classroom spaces. Thomas Ogden uses the term "analytic third" to refer to this same phenomenon (42).

An instructor's implicit, felt experience of classroom discussion as a thing that she creates with her students tends to be more palpable when something is not working than when it is. Typically, a teacher senses that a discussion is not working in a number of ways, many of which are outside the realm of cognitive understanding. Recently, Laura, a new instructor, came to me after the discussion in her third class. She had been quite happy with the first two class discussions. Almost everyone spoke. Students seemed to be digging into the difficult text and trying to figure out what it was really saying, what their interpretations were. There was tension in the room, but a healthy tension, in which students wrestled with and against each other and with and against the texts they were reading. In the third class, however, this tension was gone. In its place was a feeling of absence, as Laura described it. It felt like nothing was happening, almost as if they were not even there in the room with her. She tried asking pointed questions about the text, the kinds of questions that had worked before, and the students remained silent. She even called on some of them, but their responses were brief and perfunctory.

This went on until the end of the class. She was certain that they finally knew she was a new teacher, even that she was a fraud. Images of teachers as romantic heroes who liberate or heal their students may have contributed to Laura's initial way of thinking about herself as a failure in the classroom after the "bad discussion" (Roskelly and Ronald 54). What would *Dead Poets Society* be, for example, without Robin Williams standing on the desk urging his students to tear out the introduction to their textbooks?

Laura did not feel like Robin Williams but seemed to have entered a horror movie. She felt that she had lost control of her class and that they were going to have to suffer together for the rest of the semester. The atmosphere was terrible in that room, she said, and she could not imagine going back in there, not to mention trying to lead another discussion. As we talked, I could hear the them/me feeling that she had about what had happened. Her questions were wrong. She did not wait in silence long enough for them to respond. She had assigned a reading that was too difficult. She had not written the right responses on their first exercises for the course. She had handed the exercises back at the wrong moment. And so on. She saw herself as a failed professional; in fact, she did not see herself as a professional at all but had become victim to what Brookfield calls the "impostor syndrome," fearing she was an impostor posing as a real teacher (155).

Initially, I tried to echo back what Laura was describing. Because I knew her to be an avid tennis player, I told her of an image I had of the discussion as a game of tennis, in which she had been serving and serving and rarely receiving a return from the other side. Laura agreed and, with more energy, said, "yeah, it was as if they put down their rackets and stared at me." But why? As we explored the possibility that the students had "put down their rackets," the discussion became something that was created by Laura and her students together—a group of individuals trying to make something work.

Laura visibly relaxed, which gave us more space in which to play around with ideas about what had happened in the classroom and what might happen next, rather than thinking about the issue in terms of solving the problem. No longer a flawed teacher who lacked the ability to teach, a teacher who did not know her stuff and needed the advice of an expert, Laura began to sound like a professional herself, musing about the difficulty of teaching. Rather than trying to solve the problem, in other words, we were both trying to figure out a way to make something work in the classroom, which mitigated both the loneliness and the emptiness of the effort. We had a shared mission; we were partners trying to figure out something together.

We decided that Laura would call her own freeze frame at the beginning of the next class. Instead of trying valiantly to invent a different dynamic, she would tell the students that she had been thinking about the previous class and then relate to them what she had told me: she had gone home a little disappointed by the last discussion; she had thought that the class discussion was not up to its usual level of energy; she felt as if it had been hard for the class to get the discussion moving; and she wondered what had been going on for them as they tried to make meaning together. She would ask the students if they too felt that the class had not been up to its usual level and, if so, why that might be. Depending on how the class responded, she thought that she might include a hypothesis from her viewpoint: for her, it might have been the difficulty of the text they were reading and that the students did not seem as interested in this text as they'd been in the last, and so she found herself feeling at a loss about how to reach them. She might even share with them the image of the class as a tennis game and ask them what kind of image they had of a good discussion.

Laura's vision of how the next class would begin was related not to some trick that would help her salvage the course but instead to her determination that together she and her students would discover something that would work. When she appeared in my office next, she told me that they had indeed done this. The students had suggested an alteration to the syllabus about the amount of reading they had to do for a class in which there was also substantial writing due, and they also offered a few alternatives to the current structure of their discussions, which they felt had become a little predictable. Even after such a short time, they had become accustomed to each other and to the texts. The newness was wearing off. They seemed flattered that she had thought about the class while they were away from each other and also flattered that she solicited their input on how to improve the discussion. In addition, they were willing to admit that they had not been as prepared as they might have been, that they had slacked off because there was much work due in other courses. By the end of the discussion, Laura felt that the class had come together in a new way, strengthened by what had gone wrong and had then been repaired between them.

I would attribute Laura's success to three factors, each of which in some way expands the implicit relational dynamics of what is possible in her classroom. First, and of great importance, her image of herself as a fraud needed to be challenged before she reentered the classroom. When she returned to class with a vision of herself as a capable professional struggling with a common problem, she had more confidence, as well as a more playful attitude toward her work, and thus more room for creative movement. Second, her willingness to raise discussion as a topic itself between her and her students in a "freeze frame," to offer them opportunities to think aloud with her about what they were creating together, made space for her students to think creatively with her. And, finally, the teacher's implicit belief in a class discussion as a fluid and changing element of classroom instruction made room for that kind of discussion to emerge.

For me, the most important aspect of Laura's solution to the stagnant discussion in the third class is that it offers both the students and their teacher an opportunity to talk about their subjective experiences of the previous discussion as they are trying to understand what it might mean to create a successful discussion in the present moment. We might argue that this dialogue could as easily take place in writing, in, for example, a one-minute essay, as recommended by Angelo and Cross. This valuable exercise would not, however, bring the voices of the students into direct contact with each other in the room. It would not allow the students and their teacher to work on discussion skills even as they are conversing about them. When a teacher asks students to think about the discussion as something they are creating, to consider the discussion as something outside them, the discussion becomes an activity that they can work on together. It also provides an opportunity for students and teachers to work together as unique partners, capable of contributing something different and valuable to the interaction. When their roles are conceived of in this way, the traditional hierarchies of student/teacher and novice/expert become less important or even irrelevant. Instead, the group acts together to make something work for the benefit of all.

Boston Group researcher Edward Z. Tronick draws from nonlinear dynamic systems theory in noting that when we think about relationships as cocreated (whether they are between infants and mothers or any other individuals), we might study the "dynamic and unpredictable changes of relationship that underlie their uniqueness" (474). Inviting students to engage in this study with us focuses them on the connections between past and present—on what has happened in the classroom in the past and how knowing something about that can change the dynamic of classes to come. As these students and their teacher enter into a dialogue about the implicit relationships in the classroom, they also, simultaneously, develop their understanding of explicit, or declarative, issues, such as the current paper topic or the text they are reading.

Before I begin to sound utopian, I must say that not every teacher can repair a failed discussion by talking with her students about it. Everything depends on what has happened before, on the atmosphere that has been established in the classroom, and on what students feel they may say and do in that particular environment. It also depends on who the individual students are and who they are together, as a group. A teacher's ability to monitor, in a conscious way, the reactions that he or she has to students at any given moment gathers evidence about the implicit relationships between individual students and the teacher, as well as among the people in the classroom. This monitoring comes so naturally to most good teachers that we do not often speak about it at all. But it is what is happening when we are thinking about where to go next as a student is speaking or when we are wondering why a particular student has not spoken today or why it is that we are so irritated by what a student has just said.

As we lead discussions, we monitor the discussion with what Theodor Reik calls "a third ear" (48). We are both in the discussion, and we are watching it from outside, looking for signs of students' interest, disinterest, engagement, or boredom. We monitor the conversation even as we participate in it. We help it stay on course, but we also look for cues about its direction. Henry Smith explains that with a "third ear," the teacher can "be both fixed and free, to scan for what may be missing, to return to a point at centre, and to be alert for surprises from multiple directions" (69). Like the analyst, in other words, the teacher cultivates the ability to "listen simultaneously on many levels" (Heimann 82).

I found myself practicing my own brand of "evenly hovering attention" in the third session of a first-semester expository writing course I taught, as students discussed a section of Jon Krakauer's *Into the Wild*. For about a half hour, debate centered on Chris McCandless, who, following one of his literary heroes, Jack London, left his home, abandoned his inheritance, and ventured west toward Alaska without a map, eventually to die of starvation in an abandoned trailer. Was he a rebellious hero making a statement against bourgeois ideology? A coward, running away from his family problems? Mentally ill? Immature? The class pursued this discussion in a lively fashion. Most students pointed to evidence from the text to support their opinions of McCandless. When they cited the text, the students articulated what they saw there and how it related to their point. This was what I was trying to teach them to do: make arguments in which they made inferences from textual evidence. I sat back in my chair and watched with delight, asking a question here and there or making a connection between two comments. (One of my favorite discussion-leading activities, keeping track of the threads of conversation on the board, might, in retrospect, have prevented what happened next.)

After about ten minutes of this, I noticed that the energy of the discussion was rapidly dissipating. I knew it because I saw a student staring into space with glazed eyes, and another student appeared to have turned her chair so that she was at a right angle to the table: "half in the discussion and half out," I thought. I also knew it because I had caught myself in a flashback to an argument I'd had with a friend the day before. The flashback signaled my disinterest, and the students' stares and body language signaled theirs. It was time to gather our observations together, to make a statement about what the various interpretations suggested about how to read this text. It was time to make a connection to the writing assignment, in which students would use this evidence and other textual examples to make an argument about Krakauer's text.

How did I know when to jump in and what to do next? In the description above, I suggest that my knowledge derived in part from a physical sense of where my students were as a group and, from the vantage point of at least two of them, where they were heading. It came from an observation of where their attention was going and how they were positioned at the table. But it also came from an internal observation of my own wandering mind. We might say that we routinely monitor the discussions we lead in writing classrooms from within and from the outside. It is like embroidery or needlepoint, only you are making up the patterns as you go along, and there are at least two people involved in the project. We pay attention to our students' and our own reactions just outside the realm of our immediate attention.

When we consider the discussion as something a class is creating together, something that is both within and outside the individuals in the room, we monitor our own experiences of it for clues about how and where to proceed. If we move this to the scene of writing, one can see how useful it could be to ask students to consider their texts as both them and not them; their texts can become spaces that involve the voices of the students and those of the authors they choose to bring into their space with them. The paper, like the discussion, consists of neither the authors they have read nor the experiences of the writer but all of these in dialogue with each other. When students have a sense that something is not right in their paper, they can use this evidence as a sign that something needs to be altered, that something needs to be brought into or subtracted from its space.

As experienced teachers, we note our reactions in the classroom space to the tension when a student who talks all the time raises her hand yet again, for example, or the anger that rises up in us when a student opens his mouth and releases an audible yawn. But what do we do once we have noted these reactions? And how do we teach new instructors to pay attention and act on their own reactions without becoming paranoid—reactive to every single gesture students make in a classroom?

Halfway through the semester in the graduate course Teaching Freshman Writing, my students and I confronted this dilemma head on. One of the requirements of the course is that students lead a twenty-minute discussion of one of the readings in our syllabus. On the first day of class, I distribute a sign-up sheet and a list of suggestions for how to lead a discussion. I also include a list of the criteria by which the students will be judged: imagination, engagement with the text, authoritative management of the conversation, student-centered writing activities, and enthusiasm.

In this class session, Sharon was leading a discussion of Mary Louise Pratt's "Arts of the Contact Zone." She began by asking a string of "guess what I am thinking and I will tell you if you are right" questions. "What is the contact zone?" she asked. "Where does Pratt talk about literacy?" "What is autoethnography?" The usually boisterous class became silent. A few students attempted to answer, but Sharon was unable to channel their answers into a larger discussion. Once they had defined the terms she listed, she did not have an idea of what they should do. She seemed frozen and responded in a monotone, with few words, and moved to present another series of questions. After each question a silence descended on the room. Quickly, the silence was filled by another question.

Sensing what I thought was a look of desperation on Sharon's face and frustration on the faces of her students, and attending as well to my own feelings of anxiety and helplessness, I asked Sharon if we could call a freeze frame to discuss our progress thus far. Sharon nodded. Several students said that they felt that she had an idea of what they should say and thus felt hesitant to speak. I concurred, adding that perhaps they could assist Sharon in finding a way to ask more open-ended questions. As I finished speaking, I noticed that Sharon had begun to cry. Other students noticed too. I felt the eyes of the class on me, and I struggled internally with what to do. Was this my fault? Had I precipitated a discussion that might have evolved more naturally or, at the very least, been initiated by Sharon rather than me?

"Oh dear," I said. "I am sorry if this freeze frame upset you."

"It's not you," she said, "or anyone here. I have PMS. I always cry when I have PMS." Many of the students laughed. One woman said, "I know exactly what you mean." Another woman commented that Sharon was brave to be so forthright in front of the class. In the minute that followed, Sharon regained her composure, asked another, more open-ended question, and proceeded to manage a discussion that became quite lively. It was particularly enhanced by the comments of the women in the room, who began to take charge of the movement of the discussion. They provided examples from their own lives, made connections between quotations from the text and their experiences, and referred to each other's comments when they spoke. One woman brought up a text the students had read for the previous class, an essay by Adrienne Rich, "When We Dead Awaken: Writing as Re-Vision." She thought that the poems in Rich's essay were examples of writing from the contact zone, but she was not a big fan of the essay overall. She felt (as students often do when they read this essay) that Rich's tone was too dogmatic.

I relaxed in my chair as this discussion proceeded. Sharon was in control, and her classmates were helping her. They had become a working group, and they appeared to be enjoying themselves as well.

Sharon's PMS comment had, I believed, altered the implicit relationships in the classroom by calling attention to the fact that they were all human beings, trying to do their best in sometimes-challenging circumstances. As I smiled to myself, one of the men in the class, Kevin, joined the conversation in an animated way. He agreed that Rich was dogmatic. He said that he was particularly angry with Rich's use of Diane Wakowski's poetry as an example of feminist writing. Rich's characterization of Wakowski was, he argued, completely wrong. He provided evidence: "I know Diane Wakowski. I had dinner with her one night when she read in Oakland, California, where I was a student before I transferred here. The poet Rich describes is nothing like the Diane Wakowski I know. Diane Wakowski is a wonderful lady."

As Kevin spoke, I continued to feel content with the way the class was moving. The students were engaged in a real discussion; they were making connections between the text and their lives and had even ventured into another text for evidence for the debate. The student discussion leader had been saved and might decide that she had led a wonderful discussion after all. Buoyed by my relief, I then made a terrible mistake. I laughed aloud at Kevin's comment about Wakowski. I kept thinking about the presidential debate in which one candidate turned to the other and said, "Senator, you are no Jack Kennedy." As I laughed, others in the room joined me. After a moment, the room had dissolved into giggles and chuckles.

Kevin, however, was not laughing. He looked at me quizzically. "What are you laughing about?" I told him what his comment had reminded me of. The class looked at me, puzzled. Not one of them had heard this before. Second, they reacted to Kevin's face. He was hurt.

Suddenly, I realized that my laughter emanated more from relief than from recognition of an old memory. I had been so nervous about Sharon's discussion, particularly my interruption of it, that I had seized on Kevin's example as a ready release. In the process, I made him into an escape valve for the anxious energy that had gathered in the room and in me. The class had joined me, perhaps because they too were on edge and because I was giving them permission to laugh at this moment, just as I had given them permission to try to assist

Sharon when I called a freeze frame. I also suspected that Kevin's gender contributed to my laughter. Was it possible that I was slightly embarrassed that women's bodies had entered our discussion? Did I feel the need to assert my authority in response to a man, to show that women teachers could be in charge without having to deny that they also have bodies? At each of these moments, I held the authority in the room about as stridently as a teacher can; I authorized laughter in Kevin's case and criticism of another student in Sharon's. And my feelings of anxiety, embarrassment, and relief became the group's to manage rather than simply my own.

I realized the irony of my wielding of authority in a freeze frame attempt to save someone else's discussion in the split second that I saw Kevin's hurt face and noted the faces of his classmates, who clearly sympathized with him. So I decided that I needed to apologize to Kevin and called another freeze frame. This time I would be the one whose pedagogy was up for discussion, I said, and I encouraged all the students to comment on my disruption of the discussion. I purposely invited criticism at this point. I told my students that criticizing the instructor is very hard for students to do, that I recognized the difficulty but really thought I had hurt someone's feelings, and that I wanted them to comment on how this had happened, if they could. Jay Frankel's discussion of the internalization of the aggressor is especially useful for distinguishing the ways in which less powerful parties in relationships become (immediately and unconsciously) docile supporters of the "king" (129). In the back of my mind I realized that this conversation could lead us right back to our discussion of the contact zone. But I also recognized that I was taking control of the class again—Sharon had no authority in this situation except as the discussion leader.

The tension in the room as I called a freeze frame to discuss my laughter at Kevin was palpable. Several of the women who had come to Sharon's rescue said that they thought my laughter had hurt Kevin's feelings and disrupted the class. Kevin insisted that he was merely confused, but I feared he could not say that he'd been hurt as well. I suggested that the problem was the way I was using my authority as a teacher even though it was not mine to use at that moment in the discussion, since another student was actually in that role. I was introducing a way of being together with my students that did not correctly fit the situation. In other words, I was misreading their implicit cues about how they wanted to be taught. Many students agreed. Susan, a student who could always be counted on to say exactly what was on her mind, suggested that we correct the problem by returning the leadership of the discussion to its rightful owner. All agreed, and the contact zone debate ensued once again. My comment and the freeze frame after it were not attended to again.

This example of what might be called an "interactive error" offered opportunities for my students and me to discover and explore "new ways of being together" in the classroom, ways that expanded our understanding of each other, the course material, and what was possible for us to do in the classroom (Tronick 475). It also taught me something about how important it is to consider when to reveal observations made by my "evenly hovering attention" in the classroom. When I called a freeze frame in Sharon's discussion, my internal reactions to the discussion were not terribly productive when shared with my students, because I was not the one in charge. In addition, my attention was not really even; my students' positions in the conversation were not taken into account, and my effort to help backfired into a usurpation of two students' authority. Add to this the difficult issue of the emotional atmosphere in the classroom when the conversation is stilted or when most of the class sits in silence while a few students attempt to move the conversation along. It would seem to be a wonderful strategy to attempt to release anxiety in such a class. But to do so at the expense of one of the students is neither fair nor productive, particularly when the anxiety is also, clearly, my own.

Perhaps the most valuable lesson to be learned from this and the other teaching encounters I have described here is of one of humility and flexibility. If a teacher can listen carefully to what is happening in the classroom and respond to what is occurring there from moment to moment, she might well be able to attend to and continue to shape what is going on even as she invites the class to have a say in what that is. A class is something that students and teachers create together, so it is not the sole domain of the instructor to ensure that the discussion works. But it is the instructor's role to set up the conditions under which discussions might thrive, to monitor closely her reactions to the discussion as it is taking place, to see what she is bringing to the conversation, and to make the classroom a place where discussion of the here and now is possible. In this sense, the teacher has a role in helping students establish and explore the parameters of what is possible to be thought and said in the classroom. This is the work of an instructor especially in the very first part of a course, when a teacher demonstrates his or her willingness to, as Albert Rouzie terms it, "engage in the play" (287).

Leading a discussion becomes, in the way I describe it here, a self-consciously intersubjective experience. In other words, we are not solitary beings in conversation with other solitary subjects. Instead, we are aware of what psychoanalysts Robert Stolorow and George Atwood call the "interplay between the differently organized subjective worlds of the observer and the observed" (*Faces in a Cloud* 41–42). If we think about teachers and students as separate individuals with their own subjectivities, each participating unconsciously in the intersubjective construction of the feeling of their particular class, the class involves the subjectivities of all the individuals involved, not in the form of a simple dialogue between the two but as a creation that the individuals construct together. It is important to note that they do so asymmetrically. Stolorow and Atwood might say that teacher and student "together form an indissoluble psychological system" (64). Tronick moves beyond this meeting of the minds to argue that "each individual's state of consciousness expands as it incorporates the meaningful elements of the consciousness of the other. . . . [T]he incorporation of the essential elements of consciousness of the other by each individual expands their own state of consciousness" (Tronick 479).

And what is it that makes an element "meaningful" if not the subjectivity of the other? That is, attempting to know what is in my students' minds makes my own thinking more complex. As I monitor my students' reactions and mine in a discussion, I establish some sense of both the what and the how of our conversation, and I use this information to consider where we might next go together. Brookfield and Preskill call this a "perception check" (173). While their interest is in speakers and listeners determining the accuracy of their understanding, mine relates as much to *how* people are experiencing each other at the moment as it does to what people are thinking about.

My students' reactions provide clues to their experiences of what is happening between us; they also offer lovely mirrors of what I am contributing to the conversation. When I hear what I am contributing to the conversation, I can begin to see the forms of knowledge I am making with my students as we are making them. This makes it easier to ensure that I am not the only one whose point of view matters in the conversation. This may seem obvious, but it was not immediately evident to Laura, who took sole responsibility for the failure of her class. Not seeing the class as an interactive, cocreated experience led to the feeling that it could not move anywhere, that she and her students were to remain stuck in an impasse for as long as the semester lasted.

I remember commiserating with other teaching assistants in my first years as a teacher about the need for a bag of tricks that we could take into our classrooms with us. If our mentors would only share their tricks with us, we speculated, we would have so many strategies to try in those difficult moments in our classrooms. Over the years, I have added to my own bag and have attempted to share my tricks with the teachers that I train and supervise. But as much as we discuss techniques and strategies, I find that we become most animated when we use our own imagery to describe different ways of experiencing what it feels like in our classrooms. We seem to become inspired when we use metaphors to capture our very personal sense of what is happening between our students and us. These metaphors constitute our own conceptual tools, which include our felt experiences, and they have the same potential for understanding our work as do the concepts of "freeze frame," "evenly hovering attention," and "implicit relational knowledge" that I outlined above.

My favorite metaphor for the classroom discussion originated from early conversations about the teacher's bag of tricks. Rather than thinking of the classroom as a place in which we perform tricks or teach our students to do so, I now imagine the classroom as a space we enter with our own little suitcases. Our suitcases are special to us, even precious, and they have been with us for so long that we sometimes take it for granted that they exist at all, not to mention remembering what is in them. The contents of our suitcases are interpersonal, as in our ways of relating in a group: lively or thoughtful, strident or shy. They include our personal tastes and opinions, such as how we like the chairs to be close to each other in the circle, without extra ones in the middle, or how we like the break to occur two-thirds of the way through the class rather than halfway (so the last part flies by). They include our ways of reading, with a pen or highlighter, and our preference for reading aloud in a slow, thoughtful voice. They also include our ways of questioning: in the voice of a pensive philosopher, a drill sergeant, a talk show host, or a crafty artisan.

If we are to have successful classes, we must attend to the fact that our students come into the classroom with their own suitcases, most of which include the offerings of their previous teachers as well as those of parents, peers, and all the other important relationships and experiences they have had. Whatever we all hold in our bags, it can be the case in any classroom that some people's suitcases get opened and their contents shared much more than do others. I recall a classroom, for example, in which our instructor effectively walked into the room, dumped her suitcase on the desk, built a beautiful interpretation, and then invited us to do the same. Or how about the classroom in which the only things that matter are students' experiences? Course evaluations of such classrooms often indicate that the students wanted more guidance from the instructor. In the classroom discussion that I am trying to imagine here, students and teacher enter the room, open their suitcases onto the floor, and then experiment with and think about what they might create together. They also reflect on what they are doing as they construct it, both to name what they are doing for themselves and to determine where they will go in their future work together.

CHAPTER THREE

WHY DON'T THEY GET IT?
Transference and the Writing Assignment

> Because each composition represents a response
> to a specific "invitation" to write, the problem of many
> papers may be the fault, not of the writer,
> but of the assignment.

—Erika Lindemann, *A Rhetoric for Writing Teachers*, 213

WHEN I WAS A GRADUATE STUDENT TEACHING WRITING FOR THE first time, one of my colleagues taught me a trick about how to design a writing assignment. "Imagine what you would want to write about," he said, "and then you will know how to assign papers that you will want to read." It sounded simple, and I tried it. I wrote an assignment about conflicts of identity in the essay we were reading: Richard Rodriguez's "The Achievement of Desire." I imagined that my students' essays would discuss issues of ethnicity and subjectivity, achievement and integrity. But when I received the papers, I was stunned to find that the students had simply rewritten Rodriguez's essay in their own words. And if their attitude in the writing work-shop was any indication of their feelings about the process of writing the essays, they had not had half as much fun as I had thought they would when I drafted the assignment. In fact, they did not seem to find the assignment challenging or interesting in any way; the assign-ment was one of any number of chores that they had to complete on their journey to an undergraduate degree. In short, my colleague's the-ory of how to write an assignment was not working for me.

The problem, I decided, was not my assignment. It was situational. After all, it was not as if I relished the opportunity to write papers in the graduate courses I was enrolled in at the time. When I thought about responding to the prompt that I had written for my students, I could conceive of multiple directions to head in, various arguments I might make, elegant quotations I might use to support my case. But when I began to visualize the paper I had to write for the graduate course I was then taking in Victorian fiction, a cold feeling began to rise from my feet toward my head. My stomach tightened into a knot. What would I write about? What would my professor want to hear?

My experience as a student responding to writing assignments bore little resemblance to my experience as a teacher who writes assignments. Rather, the two roles appeared to be designed to con-flict. In my frustration, I decided that students and teachers were caught in a system of power relations in which students try to figure out what teachers want them to write, while teachers attempt to avoid being bored to tears or moved to anger as they read the papers. I would never write an assignment that was utterly enjoyable and challenging for my students, because they were operating from an assumption that they needed to try to read my mind, whereas I was trying to invite them to use their imaginations to make something I'd never seen before.

Many theorists who consider the teaching of writing from psycho-analytic perspectives might agree with my conclusion about writing assignments, although they more precisely diagnose this pedagogical dilemma as a problem of transference. Freudian and Lacanian models of classroom practices, including the writing of assignments, tend to characterize teachers as "subjects who know" and students as individuals who transfer all kinds of images of authority onto their teachers. The students try to discern what the teacher wants to hear and to produce it. Teachers, on the other hand, attempt to teach the students to think for themselves: to help students "bring unconscious thoughts to discourse" or to "work through resistance" to their own desire for knowledge (Bracher; Brooke; Finke; Jay). Teachers attempt to help students discover what they want to say, whereas students imagine one correct response that lies in the teacher.

Some psychoanalytic approaches to pedagogy explain students' attempts to please their teachers in therapeutic terms. In this literature, students occasionally appear as pedagogical patients who are "cured" by the teacher, and teachers act as blank screens onto which students project their educational neuroses (Berman, *Diaries*; Berthoff; Bracher; Brooke; Finke; Jay). These models can be very comforting for a teacher who might be tempted to think that she is failing her students because they describe the teacher as a recipient of students' transferences rather than as an agent who casts her own distortions and projections onto the students. But just as psychoanalytic models of analysts as blank screens have been replaced by the "two-person model"—that each person's subjective experience contributes to the creation of meaning in psychoanalysis—theories of teachers as blank screens do not entirely account for the interactive component of the teaching process. Students and teachers work together, with, and against each other, throughout the writing process. This is perhaps no more obvious than when students are responding to a prompt that the teacher has crafted.

What happens when we consider that the teacher is not a blank screen but perhaps an originator of transferences in the classroom? In this chapter I investigate how teachers might recognize and make sense of the ways in which they indirectly and often unconsciously shape what happens in their classrooms from the perspective of designing and explaining writing assignments. Teachers unconsciously participate in the creation and reproduction of particular forms of knowledge in a classroom, and their students are often the objects on which

these ways of knowing are projected. In the case of the writing assignment, the teacher crafts a prompt to which the student responds, then
reads the responses and comments from the perspective of one who
knows something about how the writing should be done. (Even the
term "prompt" emphasizes that the teacher originates the process.) If
student essays reflect teachers' unconscious pedagogical theories back
to them, then it is the students who suffer the consequences when
teachers cannot recognize these essays as versions of what they have
projected onto their students.

Many theorists of writing draw from psychoanalytic models to
understand the ways in which students and teachers project their
own desires, most of which are unconscious, onto each other. As I
noted, many focus more directly on the student rather than on the
teacher. Students in this literature sometimes appear as victims of
the unconscious, caught in ways of seeing and thinking that are
unknown to them; teachers, however conflicted they are acknowl-
edged to be, are described as potential liberators of their students or
even quasi therapists. When teachers and students are described as
equally conflicted parties in the classroom and teachers are not cast
as heroic liberators of their students, it is sometimes suggested that
transference can be eliminated, as if it were a matter of the participant's choice. None of these psychoanalytic readings of the relationship between the writing instructor and student provide a close
examination of teacher as subject and transferential figure in the
classroom. I attempt to do such a reading here and thereby to explore
one of the most influential factors in the design of writing assignments—the teacher's unconscious epistemological agenda. But first I
survey what we might learn from the important psychoanalytic readings of the classroom that have been published to date.

Images of the teacher as therapist and the student as his or her conflicted patient abound in psychoanalytic approaches to the teaching
of writing. Gregory Jay, for example, notes that the teacher's job is to
"bring unconscious concepts, defenses, and desires into the realm of
discourse, argument, and performance" (790). He is joined by Mark
Bracher, who believes that "there is strong evidence that a psychoan-

alytic approach to the teaching of writing can . . . help students reduce the sort of psychological conflict that not only causes them personal suffering but also contributes to writing problems and social problems" (147). Robert Brooke appears to agree, as he describes the teacher's institutional position in this simile: "The writing teacher, like the confessor or therapist, is institutionally a version of the Subject Supposed to Know" (682). These writers draw from psycho-analytic theory to focus on students' unconscious resistance as the main obstacle to learning. They tend to describe the teacher as a per-son who is institutionally authorized to unblock resistance. These writers create a picture of a teacher who knows, a teacher who acts as a kind of analyst in the classroom, and although they resist actually naming the teacher as a therapist, they illustrate the temptation for both students and teachers to imagine the teacher in this role. Their useful analyses of students' blocks and resistances to learning invite us to imagine what instructors' blocks might be.

Psychoanalytic readings of the classroom do turn to the teacher's unconscious transferences in the classroom when they begin to consid-er questions of the teacher's authority. Robert Brooke argues that stu-dents "can always choose not to enter transference by refusing to trust the authority" (682–83), while Laurie Finke discusses a student's writ-ing in a diary as breaking through "the relations among authority, mas-tery, ignorance, and resistance necessary to any real knowledge" (26). Finke and Brooke elegantly uncover students' difficulties in negotiating authority and power in writing. They identify the teacher as an institu-tional authority who can be resisted. Student writers in Finke's class-room learn to resist a teacher's authority by writing in a diary rather than a formal paper, whereas in Brooke's, a student voluntarily refuses to trust the person who makes decisions about final grades. In each of these readings of the classroom, however, the workings of a particular teacher's authority remain unexplored. The emphasis tends to be on the institutional role rather than the individual instructor.

Patrick McGee also investigates students' willingness to resist an authoritarian relationship that necessarily disempowers them, but he moves closer to considering the teacher's role in the relationship. He argues that "experience teaches us that students don't lie. They simply misconstrue. But the way into their misconstructions is a labyrinth most teachers hesitate to enter for lack of time and support. Out of frustration, they go on correcting commas, writing composition textbooks, and generally *knocking their heads against the wall of a resistance to language that may be their own as much as their students'*" (669–70; emphasis added). McGee helpfully suggests that resistance to learning (which he attributes to a resistance to language) may be both the teacher's and the student's problem, although he focuses more on students who experience the entrapment than on teachers. McGee presents a generous view of students when he argues that they "don't lie," but his use of the term "misconstructions" unfortunately presents students as the ones who repeatedly get it wrong, while his characterization of teachers knocking their heads against the wall depicts the resistance as outside them. Teachers work against these misconstructions as they write textbooks and correct commas. Brooke, Finke, and McGee bring us to the threshold of the investigation of individual teachers' uses of authority that I attempt in this chapter.

A number of psychoanalytically informed pedagogical theorists work directly against dichotomized portraits of sick students and their "therapeutic" instructors. Ann Murphy is most forthright in this effort, as she asserts that "we must recognize that we are simply not qualified to define ourselves as analysts for our students, however true it may be . . . that teaching writing elicits some of the same powerful forces of transference and resistance that psychoanalysis does" (179). Wary of Lacanian readings of the classroom, which leave out "the energies of power and authority shared by *each* role [student and teacher]" (176), Murphy suggests that we acknowledge from a Freudian perspective the role that transference plays in the classroom. Her emphasis on the role of transference as a mutual role-playing event in the classroom provides a helpful corrective to images of the teacher as a blank-screen therapist diagnosing student problems. Murphy argues that "if we understand some of the complex subtext of the student-teacher relationship, perhaps we can more effectively respond to student transference and resistance . . . by focusing directly on the problem through a mid-semester discussion of and evaluation of the student's progress, for example . . . or we might move more obliquely, directing student reading and writing onto the troubling issues of class and education" (185). Murphy acknowledges the teacher's power in the educational process, although she does not explicitly address the teacher as a subject in the classroom.

The theorists I have cited almost always acknowledge the importance of the teacher's unconscious concepts, defenses, and desires to be of crucial importance if we are to understand students' struggles in learning to write, but they do not directly examine teachers' conflicts as key to understanding students' conflicts. They do not help me to understand, for example, the entrapment I felt as a beginning teacher caught between an image of myself as taskmaster and that as liberator, or my inability to craft a writing assignment that was challenging for my students and for me. Almost as soon as I received my students' papers, it seemed to be inevitable that the students would be blamed for what I was unable to show them how to do. Gregory Jay would argue that my difficulties arose because I participate in discourses that remain invisible to me: "The student experiences his or her existence as a being subjected to various discourses, including that of the teacher" (790). But how was I to gain access to these "discourses" when they were largely inaccessible?

Whether we term them "transferences" or "discourses," gaining access to them remains a daunting and important task for any teacher. In chapter 2, I argued that a freeze frame might help us do this in a classroom discussion. But theories of transference in the classroom offer another way to approach the problem, particularly as it concerns the assignments that we design. Shoshana Felman borrows from Lacan to recommend that a teacher might *"learn from the students his own knowledge"* (33). Felman's use of Lacan suggests that she believes students have much to teach their teachers about the knowledge that is produced in their classrooms. How is a teacher to learn about "his own knowledge" from his students? The specifics of this process remain largely uncharted in the literature.

[67]

In *Writing Relationships*, Lad Tobin finds a way to analyze his agenda as a teacher by drawing from Freud's notion of countertransference. Tobin shows how a writing instructor's unexamined assumptions about good and bad writing inform his teaching practices. He describes a situation in which he reads an excellent student essay to a colleague, and the colleague is not as impressed with it as Tobin is. This encounter leads Tobin to revise his estimation of the paper, and he decides that he liked it because its "whole argument echoed [his own] ideas" and because the student made him feel confident in himself as a teacher (335). Tobin interprets this experience as paradigmatic of many teacher-student relationships, in which "countertransference—our unconscious responses to our students, or more significantly, our unconscious responses to their unconscious responses to us . . . shapes the reading and writing processes" (32).

Tobin's emphasis on the student's reflection of the teacher's unconscious processes offers a new way to understand the teacher's participation in the creation of knowledge in the classroom. His use of Freud's definition of countertransference, in which Freud characterizes an analyst's unconscious responses to his patient as obstacles to be "overcome" in continued self-analysis (quoted in Tobin 32), promises an alternate model for understanding the teacher's role in the classroom. Unlike Freud, who sees transference and countertransference as "obstacles," Tobin suggests that countertransference is necessary not to the success of a treatment but to that of a writing class: "I don't think we can have it both ways: we cannot create intensity and deny tension, celebrate the personal and deny the significance of the personalities involved" (33).

Tobin's inquiry into the ways his past experience shapes his responses to his students offers a useful way for us to examine teachers' unconscious participation in the creation of knowledge in their classrooms. But I would adjust his theory in two important ways. First, although there are personal relationships from our pasts that shape our teaching, our teaching is also shaped by our disciplinary training, which informs our ideas about what knowledge is, how it gets created, and how it might best be expressed. Second, our unconsciously held beliefs do not always surface in response to students' unconscious transferences onto us; in fact, we offer students our unconsciously held pedagogical beliefs in many interactions we have with them, verbal or written. Their responses to us are thus countertransferential in the sense that the original transferences are our own. This is most certainly the case in the design of the writing assignment.

Teachers engage in a game of transference and countertransference with their students, but at least in the case of the writing assignment, the transference begins with the teacher rather than the student. When we are bothered by our students' papers and when they do not do what we expect them to, we confront the limits of our understanding of our students, as well as, and perhaps even more importantly, the limits of our understanding of ourselves. Forced to consider how our own ways of seeing the world inform our interactions with our students and how our ways of understanding what it means to teach writing limit and shape our students' experiences as writers in our courses, we participate in a dialogue with them that we have started and the terms of which we have outlined. We also encounter a tremendous opportunity to learn something that will enlarge the dimensions of the world in which we invite students to make knowledge with us.

Whereas the theorists I cited above draw from Freud or Lacan to make arguments about transference in the classroom, my understanding of transference as originating from the teacher is informed by very recent work in psychoanalytic theory on the subjects of transference and countertransference (Mitchell; Stolorow and Atwood). Much of this work falls under the labels of "intersubjective," "developmental," and "relational" theory, and it corresponds to developments in postmodern theory in composition studies. Summarizing some more recent theories of countertransference, psychoanalyst Glen Gabbard writes, "Relational and constructivist theories . . . stress that the analyst's actual behavior influences the patient's transference to the analyst. Hence, both transference and countertransference are jointly constructed on the basis of the mutual influence of the two parties . . . countertransference and transference are inextricably linked. . . . [T]raditional model[s] of transference-countertransference may understate the analyst's responsibility for initiating a sequence of interactional events" (10–11).

When we consider how Gabbard's summary applies to the scene of writing, we might surmise that difficult or unsettling interactions between students and teachers may have been generated by the teacher. What Tobin describes can more accurately be called a teacher's transference, rather than countertransference. It is not that students initiate the teacher's response, in other words, but that the students' responses are initiated by the assignment which the teacher consciously and unconsciously designs. Thus, to analyze student papers from the perspective of recent psychoanalytic theory, we might ask this question: What is it that my students' responses to me can teach me about assignments as a form of dialogue between us, a dialogue informed in no small part by things that we have read and experienced in the past?

When writing assignments are conceived of as teachers' transferences onto our students, the student's essays become a way for us to confront and begin to understand our pedagogical theories as we hear them back through the students. Once we begin to see what we are projecting onto our students in the form of the assignment, we can enter into a dialogue about assignments with our students so that we can acknowledge more precisely and openly what we are inviting them to explore. But how can we identify the projections onto our students in the writing assignments when we construct these assignments?

Consider a writing assignment that asks students to use personal experience and at least one text to develop an argument in response to a particular question. Years ago, I asked students to use an essay of their choice and examples from their own experience to talk about a time when they changed their way of thinking about something and what the significance of that change was. I had seen the assignment in a popular guide to writing, and it seemed like fun. Like many teachers who give assignments like this, I believed that its open-endedness would be liberating and challenging, because a student might successfully write about anything, as long as the writing was detailed, clear, and compelling.

And yet many of the essays students wrote in response to this prompt were far from compelling; reading a whole stack became dreadfully boring. There were essays about not driving too fast, treating friends and dating partners with respect, and being more appreciative of one's parents. Several students narrated tales of sports injuries or losses due to impatience; a few did not appreciate a grandparent until after his or her death, and at least two reconsidered the meaning of solitude once they had gone into the woods by themselves for a few days. The responses elicited some of the most powerful clichés of American culture, and I found that I had a preference for some of these cultural clichés over others. I liked adventure stories, particularly ones about loss and recovery: a young woman's story of her father's tragic death in a mountain-climbing accident, or a young man's narrative of escape from Vietnam. My assignment reflected my own taste and interests and contained within it a bias I did not know I had when I crafted it.

When I went to graduate school, I learned to give a different kind of assignment: one that explicitly asked students to situate themselves in a dialogue with multiple texts and to use the texts to test and expand their own theories. These assignments reflected a shift in my own theoretical training, yet my training did not necessarily resolve the dissatisfaction I felt when receiving student papers. When I asked the students to discuss Rodriguez's "Achievement of Desire" through the lens of Adrienne Rich's "When We Dead Awaken: Writing as Re-Vision," for example, the students discussed Rich and then Rodriguez, or Rodriguez and then Rich. Most generalized: Rich was an angry feminist, whereas Rodriguez was a kiss-up, or both of them were whining about nothing. In those days, it was very difficult for me to design an assignment that did not elicit the pat response, no matter how hard I tried to define the parameters within which students might think critically.

That same semester, I was teaching my first basic writing course. Here the clash between my training, which was embedded in the assignment, and the assignment, which in no way explicitly stated that training, became acute. The students were writing about gender roles in Amy Tan's *The Joy Luck Club*. I had asked them to consider how gender roles influenced the decisions of any of the mother-child pairs in the novel. The students' drafts said little about gender and much about the plot. Frustrated, I stumbled upon an exercise that provided the students with an opportunity to become more aware of what I was actually asking them to do. I asked the students to restate the assignment in their own words. Invariably, I found that what students said I was asking them to do varied drastically from what I had intended.

I tried this in-class assignment with both the 101 students and the basic writing class. In the 101 class, some of the students interpreted my request that they look through Rich's eyes at Rodriguez as an exercise in fiction. They would imagine what Rich looked like, where she drank coffee, what colors she liked, and then produce a lively description of Rodriguez. Others knew that I was interested in Rich's feminist theories but did not believe that citing Rich's text was necessary to interpret Rodriguez using these theories. Still others focused more on Rodriguez than on Rich—after a cursory reference to her, they were ready to spend the rest of their time on Rodriguez's dilemma. Once we discussed their interpretations of the assignment, I became much clearer about what I was expecting from them and even projecting what they might write. And the same thing happened with the writers who were trying to interpret Tan's text.

My frustration with students' essays and subsequent dialogue with them about the assignment constituted a form of disruption and repair. In this case, the disruption signaled a gap between what I wanted students to think about and what they actually were considering in their essays. My efforts to write a better assignment were motivated by what first emerged as frustration and rage in response to my students' essays. When I asked what the students heard in the assignment, I began to attempt to repair a communication that had become faulty. I became more aware of my own transferences onto students in the form of the writing assignment and tried to produce a more effective, more explicit, assignment. This process influenced my later work as a writing program director, as I learned to hear a teacher's frustration with student writing as a reflection of the relationship between the student and teacher that was initiated by the teacher when she or he wrote the assignment.

A few years ago, an instructor of expository writing was teaching *Jasmine*, a novel by Bharati Mukherjee, to a class of fifteen students. The title character, undergoes a number of personal transformations as she moves from childhood to adulthood, from India to the Upper West Side of Manhattan to a farm in Iowa. Her name changes; she changes partners; her idea of herself changes. In her first essay assignment for the novel, the teacher asked her students to analyze the ways that Mukherjee develops Jasmine's character, using the idea of self-transformation. The teacher came to see me with a number of the resulting essays because she thought they were terrible. The students all seemed to be saying the same thing; no one was analyzing the text, and everyone was summarizing it.

One student, Alan, wrote the following response: "The second scene that changes Jasmine is in Chapter 23. Jasmine is in New York, and she is explaining the situation at the present time. She says 'with Duff in school full days, Taylor arranged a part time job for me at Columbia in the Mathematics Department answering phones. I work six hours a day, at six dollars an hour, suddenly doubling my caregiver salary. I offered to move out, which seemed the American thing to do, but Wylie begged me to stay' (Mukherjee 1989, 159). She also discusses how she looked through a catalogue on numerous different courses and so many courses in science, in art, and in other languages."

Alan collects examples of what Jasmine does in the novel to answer his teacher's question. He uses these examples to prove that Jasmine changes throughout the course of the novel. But his argument does not build or become any more complicated that that. He uses a long quotation, does not analyze it, and then moves on to another point, perhaps because he assumes that citing examples of moments when Jasmine does something different provides adequate explanation of her transformations. Essentially, the student recites the assignment back to his teacher. She says, "Analyze the ways Jasmine's character changes."

He says, "Here they are." But the student does not analyze the changes, and so he essentially summarizes the plot of the novel.

As the teacher and I puzzled over other students' similarly simplistic responses, we discussed how we might have responded to the assignment she had written. We quickly established that we both knew what it meant to "analyze" a text: we had to take what we saw in the novel and do something with it. And so, we started discussing Jasmine's multiple identities. We noted that she changed in response to different cultural codes as she traveled across America. As we spoke, we began to notice that our language was very similar. When we thought about analysis and change in this novel, we thought about changes in identity. We talked about multiple or bifurcated identities, as well as cultural codes. It became clear that we had similar ways of talking about how culture defines and subverts individual agency and community and also that our articulations were informed by conversations about texts that the students had never had.

Our realization that the students were supposed to explore positions that had not been made accessible to them clarified the problem of the assignment. This teacher unknowingly assumed that Alan's way of reading culture resembled her own. She thought she could say the words "analyze," "individual," and "culture" and he would know she meant discuss Jasmine as a "postmodern self," who works within and against "cultural constructs" to shape her multiple and fluid identities. Rather than identifying her students' plot summary and overreliance on textual examples as deficiencies in the students, this teacher looked for the ways in which that writing actually reflected limitations in her own vision as it was articulated on her assignment sheet. Upon realizing that she was expecting her students to produce analyses for which only she had the analytic tools, she began to see that her own knowledge was itself reflective of her particular institutional situation: as a graduate student at a research university with a strong emphasis on contemporary theories of the postmodern subject—a graduate student who often wrote seminar papers about multiple identities and contested spaces. She was a member of a community to which her students had no access, a community of graduate students and their teachers, of contemporary theorists and their readers. When she realized this, she found a way to reach out to her students—in this case, she extended a text, which became the subject for the next assignment.

For the fifth assignment, the teacher asked students to read Gloria Anzaldúa's "*La Conciencia de la Mestiza*/Towards a New Consciousness." She specified her agenda by providing access to theories about identity and culture that she had in mind when she wrote the original assignment questions. Providing Anzaldúa's theories of identity to her students gave them the opportunity to appropriate those theories—to make sense and then make use of them from their own particular situations. And thinking about her transferences onto the students in the form of the assignment helped her see how to do that. In the assignment, the students were to use Anzaldúa's idea about the new consciousness to explain Jasmine's inner conflicts in making a decision; they were also to use *Jasmine* to test Anzaldúa, since they needed to discuss the ways in which the author's theories did not explain Jasmine's transformations.

Here is what Alan wrote in response: "Should Jasmine feel as if America has more to offer her, or, does the fact that Taylor 'doesn't want to scour and sanitize the foreignness' make her think differently? It seems as if Taylor contradicts his own thoughts, when he tries to help Jasmine. This part of Jasmine's inner conflict is similar to Gloria Anzaldúa's discussion of being caught between two cultures. Jasmine was forced to make a decision whether or not she wanted to stay in India, or go to America. Jasmine's feelings relate to what Anzaldúa says on page 389, about juggling culture. Gloria [Anzaldúa] said that she must split culture or choose the dominant one. Jasmine needed to make a decision to become American or stay Indian, whereas Gloria [Anzaldúa] needed to find herself a new identity or as she states 'a new consciousness.'"

Alan is beginning to interpret *Jasmine* in this essay, in the process of what Kurt Spellmeyer would call "appropriation" (Common Ground 37). The student begins to read through Anzaldúa in order to interpret *Jasmine*. No longer needing to recite his teacher's assignment back to her, he has begun to develop a new way of seeing Jasmine's transformation. Anzaldúa's theory gives him the frame he needs to build his own reading of a text. Pointing out that Taylor struggles with inner conflicts about himself and Jasmine's "foreignness," even as Jasmine herself struggles with others' responses to that foreignness, the student recognizes multiple conflicts, within an individual, between individuals, and between cultures. And he is struggling between opposite ideas: is Jasmine juggling or choosing?

These issues are garbled in this draft, but his peer tutor will give him some feedback on this, and his teacher will ask him questions in the margins about his ideas when she responds to his final paper. My point is that the student could not explore such repositioning in his first essay, because his teacher's assignment did not help him to articulate a worthwhile project, a project that had some stakes for him. He needed to have the latitude to complicate his ideas about Jasmine, and he needed to be given the tools to come up with his new interpretation of the novel. He was without these tools when he responded to that first assignment. But because his teacher asked about her own role in the disappointing paper, he has new purpose. He uses Anzaldúa to develop his own position in relation to Jasmine and to the larger issues of identity and culture.

I do not think that this student has escaped his teacher's view of the world when he writes this essay. I'm not sure that doing so is ever entirely possible in a classroom. Nor do I believe he has discovered a language of his own or found his own voice, which I also suspect is never truly possible. I am arguing that we need to deal in smaller, more specific terms than these. In this situation, a teacher revises her sense of what everyone knows, showing her knowledge to be produced in a particular space and time. She realizes that what constitutes common sense for her does not necessarily constitute common sense to her students. Her revision of the assignment reveals a negotiation between herself and her students in which she realizes she is generalizing, retreats and rethinks her position, and then returns, extending the new assignment as a connection among herself, her students, and the novel they are all reading.

The example I have just discussed involves a particular theoretical approach that becomes quite obvious to the instructor through her students' unsatisfactory responses to the assignment she had written. But we do not always hold particular theories in mind when we write an assignment, even unconsciously, at least not in the sense that we can provide them to students in the form of a text. More often, we hold theories of how the assignment might be answered that have roots in our own reading and writing practices, roots that go back to our graduate training, to our own writing, and even to ways of thinking and being that have been ingrained in us from a very young age. These theories are hard to access because they are complex and embedded in our everyday habits. But they can become visible to us when we become frustrated with what we perceive to be an omission or deficiency in the writing of one or more of our students.

It is hardly unusual that our ways of reading should be so invisible to us that they do not seem like ways at all. Even when we are acutely aware of the ways that biases shape interpretations, we inevitably become caught in our own. In "Reading Ourselves: Toward a Feminist Theory of Reading," for example, Patrocinio Schweickart resists the totalizing models of reading provided by reader-response theorists such as Stanley Fish and Wolfgang Iser. She argues that these theories "overlook the issues of race, class, and sex, and give no hint of the conflicts, sufferings, and tensions that attend those realities" (529). Schweickart instead proposes a dialogic way of reading, which accounts for both the integrity of a text and the experience of its readers: "An interpretation, then, is not valid or invalid in itself. Its validity is contingent on the agreement of others. . . . That is to say, to read a text and then to write about it is to seek to connect not only with the author of the original text, but also with a community of readers. . . . Feminist reading and writing alike are grounded in the interest of producing a community of feminist readers and writers, and in the hope that ultimately this community will expand to include everyone" (545).

Correcting Iser and Fish, Schweickart emphasizes reading as a social activity involving readers and writers who differently and collectively experience all kinds of conflicts, sufferings, and tensions. Therefore, she concludes, it is impossible to assume that there is a single correct reading of a text or that one can develop a reading in isolation, without considering the opinions of others. But Schwieckart then says that feminist readers are working to produce communities that offer alternative ways of seeing the world, ways of seeing that she hopes will one day be shared by "everyone." When Schwieckart envisions a community of everyone, she assumes the naïvely totalizing position that I held when I wrote my first writing assignment about Richard Rodriguez—that one day everyone will think what she is thinking.

Recognizing the totalizing quality of models of reading like the one described by Schwieckart, Adrienne Rich (whose essay "Vesuvius at Home: The Power of Emily Dickinson" gave Schwieckart her most important example of feminist reading strategies) insists that feminists need to develop a politics of location. Rich asks, "Isn't there a difficulty of saying 'we'? *You cannot speak for me. I cannot speak for us*" ("Notes" 224). As an alternative to the totalizing "we" or the appropriating "I," Rich describes a "we who are not the same. We who are many and do not want to be the same" (225). When Schwieckart suggests that feminists will one day share a single community, she risks representing the world as inhabited by readers who are more or less like her. Teachers regularly, if unconsciously, make this same assumption when they design writing assignments for their students.

Take, for example, a typical writing assignment that asks students to use personal experience: "Talk about a time when you felt that you changed your attitude about something." Teachers who give such assignments might imagine that they are the most open-ended of all prompts. A student might successfully write about anything. Yet we have all read detailed and clear essays in response to such a prompt that do not interest us in any way. In fact, reading a whole stack of them can become tedious. We might in the end find the most fantastic or horrific story to be the most compelling. I remember, for example, finding a man's story of overcoming testicular cancer to be the most interesting of all the essays I'd received in response to an assignment asking students to "talk about a difficult experience you've had." But was it the writing that interested me, or was it the content? I suspect it was the latter.

Min-Zhan Lu suggests that "the teacher's knowledge, whether it be of the students' needs or of cultural/intellectual resources, [should be] presented to students as a discursive construct motivated by specific social interests and capable of producing specific social effects" (899). Lu argues that teachers who are able to see the ways that their own knowledge is located, and acknowledge that to their students, move away from unrealistic and undemocratic notions that students need to be rescued or acculturated. But how do we know how our knowledge is located if it is embedded in us? We might, for instance, draw from an example of a student paper and a teacher's assignment to argue that what we need to do is quite simple—tell our students what we think we are trying to teach them, and they will be more able to make choices about how and what to learn. But it is more difficult than it might seem, for our efforts to be self-critical about ourselves as teachers are inevitably hampered by our own institutional situations.

I originally intended to look at numerous published writing assignments so that we might discern what is invisible to analysis when students respond to the prompt. But without a real student to respond, a real student who has to do what is assigned, and a real teacher to say "yes" or "no" or "almost," I found it difficult to improve these assignments. This is because assignments are ultimately communications between real people in individual classrooms, and when we try to generalize about them, we fall into the trap that I fell into when I assigned Rodriguez and Tan or that the teacher who assigned *Jasmine* fell into when she asked her students to write about multiple identities. We begin to imagine what should be in the texts that our students wrote without considering the subjectivity of any writer but ourselves.

As long as we hold the final say about what is or is not in the text, what is good writing or bad writing, what is or is not an adequate response to our assignment, we specify what will remain invisible or anomalous in the teaching of writing. And we cannot escape this. But we can confront it and consider how the relationships between our own assignments and the papers students write in response provide indicators of what we are transferring onto our students in the form of the writing assignment.

A century ago Sigmund Freud explained the concept of transference as a kind of cliché: "[Transference is] a special individuality in the exercise of [the subject's] capacity to love. . . . This forms a cliché or stereotype in him . . . which perpetually repeats and reproduces itself as life goes on, in so far as external circumstances and the nature of accessible love-objects permit, and is indeed itself to some extent modifiable by later impressions" (312–13).

When we first experience love, Freud suggests, we experience it in special and individual ways. Our later experiences come to be shaped by the particular details of how we have been imprinted: how we have been loved and how we have loved in the past. When we articulate our desires for our students, in the form of assignments, we enact our own stereotypes, or clichés, to frame their experiences. So if students feel alive when they first enter a college writing classroom, might they automatically use their own clichés to articulate what they are just coming to know? This is precisely what I explore in chapter 4.

CHAPTER FOUR

"EVERYBODY HAS THEIR OWN IDEAS"
Responding to Cliché in Student Writing

Things always change . . . however, the more things
change, the more they stay the same.

—Student writer, Fall 1997

"EVERYBODY HAS THEIR OWN IDEAS." "IF WE TRY HARD ENOUGH, we will succeed." "It depends on the person." After almost two decades of teaching composition at four different universities, these clichés continue to plague me when I respond to student writing. Papers that explore the limitations on individual opportunity in the United States assert the possibility of beating the odds; arguments about multiple identities urge us to find our true selves; discussions of socially constructed knowledge conclude that we each invent our own ideas every day. How can it be that students write for pages about the complexities of institutional power, multiple identities, and situated knowledge and then refute what they have discussed in a trite or overused phrase? In this chapter I argue that teachers who become more attentive to their own clichés will find students' clichés far less disruptive. They may also develop more complex ways of thinking about student writing that will lead to more specific and more helpful marginal comments.

David Bartholomae argues that clichés (overused expressions or ideas that he terms "commonplaces") represent the safety of a world that makes sense to our students, whereas the language of the university can seem unfamiliar and strange ("Inventing the University" 138). He explains that students move away from clichés when they begin to find a voice in the conversations of the university, forsaking their acquired common sense to embrace the critical language of their instructors. The first-year composition course, according to Bartholomae, should teach students *not* to make common sense ("Reply to Stephen North" 130).

Many of our theorists and textbook authors agree with Bartholomae (Joseph Harris; Lu; Spellmeyer, *Common Ground*). Walter Ong, for example, argues that cliché is characteristic of oralist culture—that those who do not have the basic technology of writing available to store and secure their knowledge necessarily communicate in terms of simple platitudes, stock phrases and epithets, little rhymes, proverbs, and commonplaces. According to Ong, no matter how literate we become, much of our consciousness is still imbued with at least a residual oralism.

In the preface of *Rereading America*, the textbook I sometimes use for my introductory courses, the authors encourage students to become active readers to avoid clichés. They urge students to question assumptions, for example, that all individuals have equal opportunity or equal access to education and property. Students might also challenge what "everybody knows" about the American Dream or read narratives that offer testimony to the power of institutions to subvert individual freedom (Colombo, Cullen, and Lisle 1–2).

As a teacher, I take note of a developing critical consciousness when a student uses an author's language to talk about his or her life experiences or analyzes those life experiences to take exception to an author's way of understanding the world. But too often that same student cannot sustain a critical voice for very long in an essay, asserting in the final paragraph the truth of such statements as "everybody can do it if they try" or "if we ask too many questions, society as we know it will fall apart." My written responses to these overused expressions tend to reflect my disappointment, frustration, or even (as I am loath to admit) anger. What is wrong with them, I ask myself, as I grade yet another concluding paragraph riddled with clichés? What is wrong with me? What is wrong is that my own teaching practices, along with the theoretical tradition that informs them, have influenced me as much as notions of common sense influence my students' writing.

If students have a tendency to write clichés, our anger when they do so reflects a tendency to respond to them in fairly predictable ways. We identify a cliché, ask a question that leads back to the text, or point out contradictions in the argument. And although it may seem that students write in critical voices for pages to please us and then in the concluding paragraph say what they really think, this pattern bears important similarities to the hybrid discourse Brian Street describes in his discussion of literacy acquisition. Rather than speaking as outsiders or as insiders to university discourse, students "frequently maintain a number of different literacies side by side, using them for different purposes" (44).

In the pages that follow, I closely examine a few of my students' most frequently used clichés to illustrate that when we interpret clichés as merely unfortunate intrusions or weak spots in their writing, we miss opportunities to learn more about what we can teach our students and what they might be able to teach us. In the process, I discuss a few of my own clichés, acquired in seven years of professional training and over a decade of teaching composition and articulated in my comments on student papers. In each case, I suggest that when we listen carefully to clichés, we will find not complacency, naïveté, or unproductive resistance but "pragmatic adaptation . . . to the new skills, conventions, and ideologies being introduced" (44). I also suggest that teachers, like students, gesture in at least two directions when we write comments on student papers. We move forward, armed with our best efforts to hear what our students are saying. But we also move backward, in often-unconscious reflections of our own educational training, to times when we, very much like our students, played the role of the less powerful party in the dance of power that is the academic institution.

Generally speaking, my assignments ask students to work with difficult texts as well as their own experiences as they explore relationships between identity and culture in late twentieth-century America. They read Gloria Anzaldúa, for example, who describes her mestiza consciousness: a mixture of Native American, Chicana, female, lesbian, and academic identities. They encounter Richard Rodriguez's conflict between the world of his Mexican American parents and that of his Anglo teachers. They examine these authors in the context of Mary Louise Pratt's theory of the classroom as a contact zone, "where cultures meet, clash, and grapple with each other, often in contexts of highly asymmetrical relations of power" (4). Looking for examples of contact zones in the texts and in their environment, they write about the soccer field as a contact zone, or the cafeteria, the dorm room, or McDonald's. They discuss contact zones as places of conflict that are inevitable in a world where people can feel powerful and powerless in the space of a few hours or even minutes. But they also identify what Pratt calls "safe houses . . . places for healing and mutual recognition . . . [places] in which to construct shared understandings, knowledges, claims on the world that they can then bring into the contact zone" (17). In contact zones, writers identify many competing cultural voices. In safe houses, marginalized groups come to identify which of those voices they might truly call their own.

I first began to think seriously about uses of cliché in student writing when students in a developmental writing class at Rutgers University seemed to enter both contact zones and safe houses in the same pieces of writing. The students were mostly working-class and around eighteen years old, and about half spoke a language other than English in their home. When we discussed the course readings in class, we debated whether the authors had any relevance to their lives. Before we could debate, we struggled to understand what the essays said, to hear the authors' words, and then to "talk back." We broke the essays down and found the pieces that made sense to us. Soon, students began to discuss the value of terms such as "mestiza consciousness" when they wanted to talk about themselves as students, workers, daughters, and sons. But they always worked with and against Anzaldúa's term, often agreeing that they had a mestiza consciousness but that it was not as contradictory as Anzaldúa describes. They also explored the interplay of race, ethnicity, home, and school in the formation of identity in the second assignment, which was to examine Rodriguez's "Achievement of Desire" through the frame of Anzaldúa's text. What did Anzaldúa help us to see in his essay? How did her essay teach us to read Anzaldúa differently? Many argued that Rodriguez was far less comfortable with a mixing of the academic and familial self than was Anzaldúa, or that Anzaldúa's understanding of the mixed consciousness was actually closer to Rodriguez's than we might suspect.

By the time the students had written the third assignment of five, I noticed a familiar pattern in their responses. First, they would use the concepts offered in the text to interpret other texts and their lived experiences, and then, they would conclude their interpretation with a clichéd final paragraph that contradicted everything they had said. The third assignment asked students to begin to develop a theory of the role of gender in identity formation as they drew from their own experiences and two texts: Alice Walker's "Beauty: When the Other Dancer Is the Self," and Jamaica Kincaid's "Girl." Many students struggled between theories of an autonomous self that exists outside of culture and a self that is influenced by gendered cultural codes. But the essays unanimously concluded with statements such as "we are all equal," "we can be whoever we want to be," and "we have to admit we have made progress."

When I first read these essays, I believed they contained moments of critical thinking and moments of complete acquiescence to the commonplaces of our culture, moments when the students struggled with Walker's and Kincaid's stories about gender discrimination and moments when they refused to listen to them. In keeping with what I had learned from Bartholomae's "Inventing the University," I attributed these contradictions to what I assumed about developmental writers: they were initiates into the university community who needed far more experience before they could write convincing and coherent critical arguments. This theory appeared to be confirmed when I asked the students why they wrote these clichés; most were unable to talk about how their conclusions differed from anything else they had written. One student, however, asked, "Isn't the conclusion the place for our ideas?"

This student's reply to my question made me realize that my faith in Bartholomae's model of the classroom produced a deficit model of their writing. I believed that their critical thinking stopped when they reached their concluding paragraphs, which echoed with cliché. My student's comment about "her own ideas" suggested a different way of understanding a cliché-ridden final paragraph, however—as a way of honoring prior lessons in good writing and as an opportunity to resist the new ideas of good writing espoused by their college composition instructor.

If these paragraphs were places for "their own ideas," perhaps my students were, without entirely realizing it, making a political move, going as far as possible into the realm of critical thinking without finally and completely selling out by asserting themselves in the most privileged space of the essay—the ending. Perhaps they said what they believed I wanted to hear and then, with the implied permission of their previous instructors, reserved a small space for what they truly wanted to say at the end of their essays. If so, they were not simply inexperienced in my language but instead wrestling to make sense of what they read in terms of what they knew and believed.

A contact zone always exists between a teacher and her students, a zone in which they can be graded and the teacher can grade, in which they represent student culture, and the teacher, academic culture. Student papers, written in this zone, reflect the imbalance of power. But in a classroom where students are readers of one another's work, a student essay might also offer a "safe house" for students to attest to the power of what they have always known (Pratt 17). If student writers insisted on the notion of the unique individual after having explored Walker's description of masked and distorted identities, for example, perhaps they were reluctant to forsake the commonplace that every human is unique and uninfluenced by other voices. Or, if they wrote that "everybody has their own ideas" after discussing Jamaica Kincaid's description of her entrapment in the opposing worldviews of her mother and father, it could be that they wanted to assert their own power to be themselves, apart from their parents and teachers.

From a formal perspective, if students wrote clichés against the inclinations of their present teacher's model of good writing, they might attest to definitions of good writing that preceded those they were learning in college. If these final paragraphs resisted the powerful voices of their teacher and the writers in their textbooks, in other words, the same paragraphs expressed solidarity with fellow students in the class, fellow writers who have felt the judging eyes of professional readers on their work, and even other teachers who have taught them ways of thinking that conflicted with the readings in their college textbooks.

One student, Andrea, discussed Walker's and Kincaid's depictions of relationships between race, gender, and identity, reaching the conclusion that "everyone has a different way in finding out who they are, but at the end we all have a way of realizing it, and hopefully are content with the results." Initially, I dismissed Andrea's conclusion as a retreat into the false certainty of one who has stopped asking questions of herself and the text. I attributed this retreat to the fact that Andrea had reached the bottom of page 4 of her essay and, having met the requirements for the assignment, could stop writing about conflicts between women's desires and the standards for self-realization in a patriarchal culture. In the margin, I asked her how Kincaid and Walker expressed their contentment and where, if ever, they expressed discontent. My other comments directed her to moments when she was questioning relationships between identity and cultural codes, when, earlier in her essay, for example, she noted that Kincaid's speaker in "Girl" could not separate her mother's voice from her own. I encouraged her to spend more time investigating what she said there about women confronting difficulties in becoming somebody other than the type of person the cultural stereotypes prescribe, as when she discussed how mothers speak those cultural codes when they demand polite behavior and sweet talk from their daughters.

Turning my attention away from what I saw as a clichéd and therefore safe conclusion, I could not see that Andrea gestures in two equally important directions in her final lines, that her conclusion actually enters a contact zone even as it rests in a safe house. On the one hand, she contests the formulation of identity as totally determined by culture by insisting on individuality: "everyone has a different way in finding out who they are." With this statement she carves out a space for each woman to realize, differently, her place in the world. On the other hand, she expresses solidarity with other women, the "they" of "everyone has a different way," speaking to the experiences of multiple women who have struggled to find a place in a sexist world. Perhaps Andrea did not contradict herself when she celebrated individual freedom at the same time that she discussed restrictions on it but, instead, worked out an "I" who is also part of a "we": as Adrienne Rich says, "We who are many but do not want to be the same" ("Notes" 225).

If Andrea wrote clichés despite my resistance to them, it is not because she did not understand the questions I encouraged her to ask; rather, having reached the age of eighteen, she had already contained and confronted a multitude of contact zones and safe houses that needed to be negotiated in any assertion of self. If one zone is that between teacher and student, another is certainly between mother and daughter. A young woman who writes that "hopefully we are content with the results" might very well address her mother, who she hopes will be content with a daughter who chooses not to conform to certain gender stereotypes, or even her teacher, who she hopes will be content with the results of several drafts in this final essay. If so, Andrea uses a cultural commonplace to say something about women her age, about how her identity might exist separately from her mother's, from that of the daughter in the Kincaid essay, and from her teacher's. The commonplace expression can alert us to the ways in which mothers exercise the power of cultural stereotypes when they raise daughters and the ways that teachers can stereotype students (or their clichés) when they respond to papers. It can also address the particular situations of women Andrea's age, who, like Andrea, yearn for places to claim as their own.

Simultaneously testifying to her experience of the world (and that of her peers) while contesting her parent's or teacher's potential to devalue these experiences, a student such as Andrea performs a critique of the culture of the classroom in her use of a cliché. In that contact zone, a teacher's voice can be heard much more loudly than can that of a student. Mae Henderson, a critic of black women's texts, explains how relationships between speakers and listeners can produce resistance and solidarity simultaneously. She describes the rhetorical situations of black women who struggle to speak in a world that has historically oppressed them in terms of both gender and race. They witness solidarity with those who have been similarly oppressed, even as they must contest a historical legacy of abuse. Black women writers recognize a history of gender oppression when they speak to black men, for example, even as they testify to a shared history of racial oppression. When speaking to white women, they articulate solidarity in terms of patriarchal domination of women and resist a history of racial oppression. Henderson notes: "Through their intimacy with the discourse of the other(s), black women writers weave into their work competing and complementary discourses—discourses that seek both to adjudicate competing claims and witness common concerns" (24).

Henderson does not write about a multicultural classroom, but her theory enabled me to hear even more of a range of possible meanings in the texts of my students who typically describe the American educational system as a system without their interests in mind. Students address competing external and internal audiences in the struggle to articulate what it means to have an identity in contemporary America. The student who asserts the possibility of an independently determined self, for example, but then argues that no individual can completely abandon her family in forming an identity, expresses solidarity with her family even as she resists ideas that families influence children's identities. Or the student who insists on the inherent value of context even as he contends that every viewer perceives the world in his or her own unique way testifies to a world based on fact even as he resists the limitations of such a world. And although Henderson's theory might explain it in far more sophisticated language than any of the students I have quoted thus far, I have no doubt that student writers attest to the reality of a world in which they are silent witnesses to powerful others as well as powerful theorists and spokespeople in their own right.

Simultaneously witnessing and resisting, giving testimony and taking exception to the way people represent reality, Andrea's classmates also challenged theories of identity that had become familiar to me. Jabari responded to the third assignment with a call to arms: "From these passages one can conclude that the reason people allow the dominant culture to shape their identity is because whites have better chances in society. While environment, personal, and dominant cultures are three factors that can contribute to identity-formation, one should value the specific culture of their family, and prevent the dominant culture from forming their identity."

Jabari's presentation of the power of the family to resist the dominant culture echoed the plea for family values in any number of campaign slogans in recent years. In the margin, I asked him to consider how Walker and Kincaid represent parent-child relationships, to compare that with the mother's perception of her daughter in the Kincaid essay, and to consider his own experiences as a son of very strict parents. Although my comments did not overtly say so, I suspected that Jabari needed to consider the ways in which he had become the property of conservative ideology when he wrote that cliché. I wanted him to question his blithe assertions of the importance of family as mimicry of a party line. But as I thought more about it as Henderson might, I wondered if, in these lines, he had attempted to contest the dominant culture and to testify to his solidarity with the culture of his family. Read this way, a family is a site of resistance, even if its call for family values is a conservative trope. Perhaps Jabari wanted his audience to value the specific cultures of their families and to resist the dominant culture's emphasis on particular kinds of families on television, for example, and the racism that those representations evoke.

Jabari's final paragraph raises interesting questions about how a student locates himself in discourse. He acknowledges that neither the relationship of one person to culture nor the relationship of one student to academic discourse is an inside/outside situation. Instead, he suggests that one simultaneously joins and resists multiple communities in an effort to establish identity. His reference to dominant cultures, for example, resists implications that family values are the same, regardless of one's race or ethnicity. Resisting the dominant culture while acknowledging its power, witnessing his participation in it while retreating into another identification (with his family), he reminds us that he is not just a student negotiating a space for himself in academic discourse. He is a person with a history; he is an active social agent in a field of competing claims on him as an individual and a member of a culture.

Brian Street's research on literacy acquisition suggests that "people frequently maintain a number of different literacies side by side, using them for different purposes" (44). His analysis explains the persistence of one of the clichés I have always found most confusing in a course that asks students to think about central myths of American identity: the assertion that the American Dream continues to be attainable for anyone who tries hard enough. This cliché appears at the end of essays in which students write about the power of social forces to hold people back from realizing their dreams or to prevent people from even conceiving of those dreams. Leo, a third student in Andrea and Jabari's class, warned that "when you are starting to question who you think you are, take a step back and see the whole picture. Realize that the key to your happiness is your identity. Discover your own American Dream." I believed that his final lines evaded a complicated issue, that he did not have a voice of his own but instead was echoing one of the primary myths of American culture—that of the possibility of individual success despite the limitations of material circumstances.

My comments on Leo's essay, like my comments on many of his classmates' essays, advised a return to the texts for further complication and clarification. I asked him to question the extent to which Walker's speaker was able to do whatever she wanted and then to think about the limitations the mother in Kincaid's essay places on the girl's possibilities for worldly success. I asked him to reconsider his final lines from this perspective. Since then, I have considered other possible readings of Leo's final lines. For example, it is conceivable that Leo's suggestion that we "take a step back" testifies to the positions of immigrants, like himself, who have formed ideas of the American Dream from afar. Perhaps his statement protests against the formulation of individual opportunity even as it appears to mimic it; it locates him in a safe house of communal experience even as it enters him into a contact zone of those who do not have equal access to this experience.

If we equate Leo's assertion of the American Dream with those of his classmates, who often express a similar position, we foreclose his negotiation between his position in the world and that of others. I believe it is more likely that he would step back toward the complications that he introduces in the possibilities for individual achievement in this culture if he investigated his connection to others who are "one step back" from the American Dream. This question allows him to return to the safe house of communal experience to gather material for entry into a contact zone. Later, he might analyze the American culture's discourses of opportunity and success, but first he needs to find spaces in which to explore the common assumptions of communities from which he does not feel excluded.

In an article about Latin American testimonial, Doris Sommer offers some insight into what my students may have been working at in their essays when she questions the ways that testimonial has been equated with autobiography. She argues that the "I" of a testimonial is very different from an autobiographical "I." Instead of referring only to herself when she uses the first-person pronoun, the woman who writes a testimonial refers to a collective self: "It would be a mistake uncritically to attribute intimacy and individuation with the first person singular pronoun in testimonials. . . . When the narrator talks about herself to you, she implies both the existing relationship to other representative selves in the community and potential relationships that extend her community through the text" (118).

Sommer's definition of an "I who is also a We," like Rich's "We who are many but do not want to be the same," can apply in reverse to the clichés I cited previously. Sometimes, I think, a student uses a cliché to refer to a "we" who can also be an "I." In other words, I am not convinced that a student who says "everybody has their own ideas," for example, has entirely absented herself, hiding her voice, as Linda Peterson has found, "within the clichés . . . of a subculture" (180). Instead, I suspect that the cliché can signal testimony to a different kind of power for a student: testimony to her participation in the multiple communities against and within which she defines herself.

Ironically, the simultaneity of an "I" who is also a "we" resounds in the error in the pronoun agreement in the cliché "everybody has their own ideas" or in "everyone is beautiful in their own way." How many times have you changed these phrases to say "everyone has his or her own ideas" or "everyone is beautiful in his or her own way"? In a personal correspondence, Richard E. Miller points out that his students do not say "everybody has their own ideas" but rather "everybody has a right to their own ideas." Although they do not mean the same thing, each of these phrases expresses a student's desire to preserve something of herself or himself in the process of writing a college essay.

Although it is not standard English, "everybody has their own ideas" suggests that the individual and the community are continuous. When we correct the phrase to say that everyone has his or her own ideas (our own cliché?), we assert the autonomy of the individual subject that contemporary pedagogical theories work hard to resist. Perhaps this error in pronoun agreement reminds us that our students speak a language that bears important similarity to Latin American testimonial, what Sommer calls "a colonized language that does not equate identity with individuality," whereas our own language can, despite our best intentions, bear a striking resemblance to a colonizing force (111).

I want to make it clear that I do not think we should celebrate errors in pronoun agreement and clichés as if they were our students' most brilliant utterances. But I would like us to consider that the places in our students' essays that most annoy us because they seem so uncritical are also places where individual students (much like their teachers, as I argue further on in this chapter) are working hard to make sense of a world in which they are always both insiders and outsiders, both individuals and members of conflicting communities. As Kurt Spellmeyer says, "The speaking 'I' does not exist, then, as a fully defined set of roles. . . . Instead, the writer must actively create a role in the breaks and spaces afforded by the game at any particular time" (*Common Ground* 71). Spellmeyer argues for a hermeneutic understanding of knowledge acquisition through which students acquire knowledge in a dialogic process, moving from what they know to what is unfamiliar and then back to a new version of their previous knowledge. In the above examples, my students constructed an understanding of my language but remained fluent in their own even as they fused these disparate literacies into another, more personal and usable version.

I am suggesting that we imagine multiple audiences for students' seemingly simplistic formulations because I want to draw your attention to what I was prepared to hear and compelled to ignore in student writing. Many researchers in the field of composition focus on this pedagogical unconscious, the process by which we make our students invisible to us. Laura Gray Rosendale, for example, notes that the popularity of the contact zone model of teaching writing produces its own limitations of vision for contemporary writing instructors. Joseph Williams explains that institutional hierarchies can produce our responses to student writing. He provides compelling evidence that the sudden fierce blast of anger that characterizes so many of our responses to student writing suggests that we see ourselves as civilization's gatekeepers, and thus error makes us want to sound the alarm and exile the perpetrator. When errors are committed by people we consider to be insiders, we usually do not even see them.

Speaking about philosophy and education, William James reminds us that our capacity to see depends largely on position: "The subject judged knows a part of the world of reality which the judging spectator fails to see, knows more while the spectator knows less" (6). When we take the position of a judge, as when, for example, we grade our students' essays, we can see only what is possible from that position. As authors of work to be judged, our students necessarily (and often very quietly) see things we cannot. And although we may argue that we avoid the most power-ful position in the classroom when we assign multiple drafts, portfolio reviews, and ungraded writings, in any class in which students receive a final grade for the course, we have the last word.

Many writers in our field discuss how we should encourage students to reflect on their cultural positions and to reposition themselves in relation to what they read and write. These writers describe class-rooms as places of conflict and struggle and routinely examine the competing voices students encounter when reading and discussing texts. Although increasing attention has been focused on teachers' negotiations of the conflicts in their classrooms, with few exceptions (most notably Richard E. Miller), these articles do not refer to student texts and teachers' specific comments on those texts as voices from "the contact zone." Produced in institutions that demand numerous sacrifices and risks of the self from the moment one enters college and in a culture that pulls on professionals no less than students, teachers' comments and students' papers can come to assume comfortable forms. We produce these forms—the commonplaces of our own par-ticular classrooms—no matter how vigilantly we attempt to pose meaningful questions, encourage multiple responses, and listen care-fully to what students are saying.

Richard E. Miller suggests that teachers might be predisposed to misread student writing because institutions do not train us to think about our own positions as teachers, and so student essays become sites "where error exercises its full reign or . . . where some untutored evil shows its face" ("Fault Lines in the Contact Zone" 395). Teachers respond this way, argues Miller, because they consider stu-dents as makers of error who need to be corrected or as believers in immoral or improper ideology. Unlike the teachers Miller describes, I learned (first as a graduate student and then as an administrator in the writing program at Rutgers University) to respect students as equal, although less experienced, colleagues in the critical conversations of the university. The graduate course in teaching composition and the program directors encouraged me to think of "error" as a breach of etiquette or as a way of speaking that differed from my own. Likewise, I learned to identify the places in their papers where students began to make sense of the relationships between their lived experiences and the textual worlds they encountered in their writing class, where they used the language and concepts from one text to understand another. Nonetheless, as this chapter attests, I still found weaknesses to despise in student writing. Mary Louise Pratt explains why this may happen despite the most careful and intellectually sound training: "When linguistic (or literate) interaction is described in terms of orderliness, games, moves, or scripts, usually only legitimate moves are actually named as part of the system, where legitimacy is defined from the point of view of the person in authority—regardless of what other parties might see themselves as doing" (14). The student essays I read were legitimate when they corresponded to what I knew about good writing: that it makes connections between texts and between text and world; that it raises questions and problems and complicates the received ideas that come to us through the media and elsewhere. When those essays did not do these things, I believed my students needed to be gently nudged into critical thought.

I remember my relief at seeing the classroom described as a place I recognized when I read Min-Zhan Lu's description of trying "to help students recover the latent conflict and struggle in their lives which the dominant conservative ideology of the 1990s seeks to contain" (910). My relief revealed my entrenchment in another ideology, an institutional ideology that had become so natural to me that I perceived it as common sense. Rereading Lu's statement and my students' clichés through Pratt's eyes makes me aware that I produce my own clichéd responses to students' essays about identity: either a student mimics the ideology of the dominant culture, or she questions it. When she questions it, she is thinking critically. When she mimics it, she is a puppet of her culture. Because my way of reading has become so natural to me, many of my students, as Miller predicts, become emblems rather than individuals, purveyors of a conservative ideology that I find simplistic and reductive.

I know very well that my students' experiences of the world are not mine and that my theories of identity construction do not now and cannot ever account for or readily explain their experiences. Nonetheless, I suggest that they can when I comment in the same basic direction on every cliché I read. In addition to my training in graduate school, my experiences of theories of identity can be traced to my history as a child of Irish and Ukrainian/Polish working-class parents, as a woman born in the 1960s who went to Catholic schools through college, and as a woman who has learned which parts of herself to conceal, and which to accentuate, if she hopes to succeed in American academic culture. I learned in my home, for example, to pursue conflict as often as possible, and with gusto, whereas in school it became clear that remaining neutral would make it easier to fit in with my peers.

Nicholas Coles and Susan Wall's astute analysis of the essays of working-class writers suggests that students may have compelling reasons for holding on to clichés such as the American Dream or the myth of individual opportunity: these students need to believe that education will help them to become successful in a world of dwindling economic opportunity. Thomas Newkirk similarly discusses cultural commonplaces in personal writing as tools of personal agency in the culture at large—tools that students have used successfully throughout their lives. Although these writers do not discuss teachers' own clichés, their articulations of students' purposes in writing clichés might apply to our own habits of responding to student writing.

Newkirk argues that "a student who writes a cliché is expressing a belief in a code of conduct that has paid off handsomely" (46). Like these students, we instructors learn codes of conduct in our graduate training and in every interaction we have with those who judge our work. Our fluency in these codes can "pay off handsomely," as our degrees, publications, and awards attest. But just as students' clichés gesture in at least two directions, I wonder if our preference for mul-

tiple meanings and critical thought over cliché reflects our resistance
to authority figures who have urged us toward the same clichés from
which our students have benefited. How many of us, for example,
have felt belittled by gendered codes of behavior? How often do we
speak of having been bound by silence to painful family values? If so,
critical thought is a kind of safe house for us in the same way that
cliché can be for our students.

Lester Faigley argues that "students will be judged by the teacher's
unstated cultural definitions of the self " ("Judging Writing" 410). He
is responding to "expressivist and rationalist traditions of teaching
writing that deny the role of language in constructing selves" and
"recommending a pedagogy that analyzes cultural definitions of the
self rather than promoting individualism" (410). It is interesting to
me that now that many of us devote most of our classroom time to discussing exactly what Faigley recommends—the "role of language in
constructing selves"—our students are no less "judged by [our] unstated cultural definitions of the self." In this case, the culture is the institutional culture in which we have learned and taught for most of our
adult lives, and the self that many of us define for students in our
comments is a poststructuralist self (much like the selves I imagine for
them in my analyses of their writing that I have discussed).

I do not celebrate authentic voices in student essays, as do the
teachers Faigley critiques. I frown on black-and-white judgments,
embrace oppositions, and celebrate multiple selves and voices. Like
Peter Elbow, I believe "it is possible to make peace between opposites
by alternating between them" (*Embracing Contraries* 68). I am much
more likely to praise a paper that describes or, preferably, decon-
structs oppositions, a paper in which meanings are multiple and pro-
liferating rather than simplistic, a paper in which a student asserts
conflicted, constructed, or multiple identities rather than a unified
one. And yet I am no less guilty of what Faigley identifies—judging
my students by my relatively unstated definitions of the self.

If my revisions of my previous interpretations of students' clichés
have taught me any specific lessons about teaching writing, these lessons relate most to my understanding of what it is I have to teach my

students. What are the unstated rules of my pedagogy, and how do they influence my ability to recognize what my students are trying to say? Put another way, my revisions have brought me to new understandings of what my training prepares me to hear and compels me to ignore in my students' writing. My strong preference for Pratt's theory of the contact zone, for example, cautions me to question what kinds of writing it values over others and why. What do these strengths and limitations imply about the utility of the theory? Did contact zones hold more interpretive power before they appeared in nearly every third article I read? In my responses to a recent batch of student papers, for example, I forced myself to pay more attention to the moments when, it seemed to me, the students entered neither contact zones nor safe houses in their papers. What I found were more possibilities for revision and also more questions—I found myself on very shaky ground, and yet I wonder if this is where my students find themselves much of the time as readers and writers.

If my graduate training had been different, I believe that I would now plead with you to try a new way of responding to student writing, one in which we simply ask our students what they are thinking about as they write the phrases that most offend us. Invoking the students' experiences as an alternative to the teacher's theories, I would perform a common interpretive move in our field. "We could know so much more about them if we asked and listened carefully," I might tell you. Although I think that heeding this advice will certainly result in useful data for future responses, I also believe that there are two major problems with doing only this.

First, the practical: who of us has the time to consult our students about every word they write in a paper, given our teaching loads, the late hours during which we often read our students' essays, and the reality that each stack presents not one but many moments of frustration for us? Second, and more important, I believe, is that this gap between our students and ourselves, like the gap between every writer and reader, can never fully be bridged. This is the nature of human communication—the fact that language writes us as much as we write it. What can always (with every paper we read) be addressed, however, are the reactions that our students' writing elicits in us, and what those reactions reveal about our most fervent beliefs as to what is possible and desirable for them to say. Having discovered this, we might decide if the knowledge is adequate or if there is some opening for a revision of our own interpretive processes.

Human social interactions, which include those between students and teachers, are never either conflict-ridden or entirely safe and nurturing. Instead, they are always both. If our students testify to their solidarity with others even as they struggle to position themselves against what seems unfamiliar or frightening, then our comments must address these contradictions without foreclosing the possibility of transformation. Unni Wikan, an anthropologist who records her study of the Balinese in *Managing Turbulent Hearts,* gives us a richer perspective on this issue when she states that "everyone's sitting room is feared by someone": "This space which is protected and private to me is another's threatening and exacting 'public': the guest fearing for her life is vulnerable and must exercise as much caution as anybody 'on display' in public. . . . [The] sitting room has multiple connotations: of safety and danger, protected space and exposed arena, intimacy and warmth but *also* of caution and restraint. Which ones will be foremost depends on situational and biographical factors" (55).

One of our goals as we respond to student essays is to pay very close attention to what students have written, keeping in mind that we cannot (and perhaps should not) know everything about students' "situational and biographical factors" when we read their work. But we can attempt to know ourselves (and our interpretive frames) better in order to help them imagine the shapes their essays might take in the revision process. Our own situations and histories can tell us a lot about how we respond and why we say the things we do on student papers, and they can also help us understand the reasons for what we perceive as our students' limited vision.

Our challenge is to learn to recognize our own clichés, the marginal comments, and the habits of thought embedded in them that have become so familiar to us that we think of them as common sense. We need to look no further than the places that most offend, frustrate, or annoy us in student writing to find clues for how to read our own ideology as it presents itself in response to our students' work. Any interpretation of what they say reflects a delicate negotiation between what our training and experiences have prepared us to hear in student writing and what a student is actually trying to say. If we imagine that the textual relationship between student writers and their teachers proceeds in the same way as a human conversation, teachers who acknowledge the beliefs they bring to the conversation are equipped to listen to their students more carefully than are those who hold their beliefs so closely that they can no longer see them as beliefs. And the best indicators of these beliefs, if we can bear to examine them, exist in our responses to students' most irksome utterances.

CHAPTER FIVE

LESSONS FROM POETRY AND PSYCHOANALYSIS
Negotiating Authority in the Classroom

I

Clear water in a brilliant bowl,
Pink and white carnations. The light
In the room more like a snowy air,
Reflecting snow. A newly-fallen snow
At the end of winter when afternoons return.
Pink and white carnations—one desires
So much more than that. The day itself
Is simplified: a bowl of white,
Cold, a cold porcelain, low and round,
With nothing more than the carnations there.

II

Say even that this complete simplicity
Stripped one of all one's torments, concealed
The evilly compounded, vital I
And made it fresh in a world of white,
A world of clear water, brilliant edged,
Still one would want more, one would need more,
More than a world of white and snowy scents.

III

There would still remain the never-resting mind,
So that one would want to escape, come back
To what has been so long composed.
The imperfect is our paradise.
Note that, in this bitterness, delight,
Since the imperfect is so hot in us,
Lies in flawed words and stubborn sounds.
—Wallace Stevens, "The Poems of Our Climate"

IN THE LINES ABOVE, WALLACE STEVENS TRACES RELATIONSHIPS between language, the self, and imperfection in human experience. No matter how "fresh" and "simple" our experiences seem, Stevens suggests, there is still the need to pin them down in words, which are "flawed" and "stubborn." Given our insatiable desire, the nature of our never-resting minds, and our inability to get the words right, we have only one option: to embrace the imperfect as "our paradise." And once we have embraced the imperfect as our paradise, its bitterness becomes more and more compelling. "The imperfect is so hot in us" that it becomes a kind of insatiable desire in itself. Getting it wrong, Stevens offers, is what it means to have a human mind. And the working mind provides its own delight.

Although we might develop an interpretation of "Poems of Our Climate" as a representation of relationships between poetry, epistemology, and desire, I am attracted to what Stevens's ideas about imperfection can teach us about being with students in the classroom. Could the imperfect classroom be a teacher's paradise? In the previous chapters, I argued that when things go wrong in the writing classroom, we have an opportunity to uncover our own pedagogical common sense, which can become almost a cliché to us because it is so familiar. Now I would like to venture beyond the limits of the writing classroom, to an exchange between a poet and a graduate student and into a conflict in a classroom at a psychoanalytic institute. In each of these examples, the person who occupies the role of instructor learns how his or her need for perfect certainty can silence students and stall the making of meaning in the classroom.

In the examples I will offer, the person who occupies the role of student directly challenges the world view of the authority figure who plays the role of teacher. These "students" are also experts in their own right, and they challenge authority figures who appear to be quite willing to question themselves and their uses of power in the interest of mutual understanding. While the "students" in these examples explicitly challenge some of the most common representations of learners—that they are passive, ignorant, or powerless victims—the "instructors" answer the challenge by stepping out of roles that cast them as all-knowing, objective, or even tyrannical. These lessons from beyond the writing classroom offer, in metaphor and story, a vision of teaching and learning that is much more about negotiation and recognition of the other than it is about getting it right. In the process, the student is revealed as a force promoting mutual understanding in the classroom through a direct confrontation with the limits of the teacher's subjective experience.

We might argue that every teacher knows that the classroom is anything but perfect and that humility, respect, and intellectual engagement should be business as usual in any classroom. After all, it is a place in which individuals from every background, with all kinds of experiences, come together. And yet it has been my experience that open dialogue in the classroom is not often possible, despite the best intentions of very knowledgeable and considerate instructors. Students and teachers, to some degree or another, crave the certainty of a world in which everything makes sense, a world in which the facts can be explained. But yearnings for certainty can limit the potential for creative exploration in the classroom.

Parker Palmer argues that a classroom organized around certainty "portrays truth as something we can achieve only by disconnecting ourselves, physically and emotionally, from the thing we want to know" (51). Perhaps our pull to the objective point of view in a classroom harkens back to our earliest training in classrooms that introduced us to the idea of education as a disembodied experience, a disciplining of the self in the service of the institution (Foucault 1975). Because we learned to experience the facts as fixed and immutable when we were young, teachers and students are pulled to locate absolute truths in their pursuit of even the messiest human questions. It makes sense, then, that the best-intentioned efforts to provide egalitarian methods of instruction can lead, as we shall see in the following examples, to moments of disconnection for students and instructors from both the material they are exploring together and each other. Repairing these connections becomes, in these examples, "our paradise."

It was November 1991, and I had been asked to introduce Sharon Olds at Boston College. She was my favorite poet, and introducing her was all the more thrilling because her poetry was the focus of one chapter of the dissertation on which I was working. It also made it all the more disappointing when, a few months after the introduction, she wrote to tell me that I had misread her work. I had cited four Olds poems in my introduction, including "What If God." In my remarks about the poem, I identified the speaker as a survivor of mother-daughter incest. Olds wrote that she had never heard the poem read that way. My interpretation so concerned her that she had considered rewriting it. She enclosed a draft of the revised poem, which she said was just for me, and that she did not think it would be published.

When I received the letter and the poem, I was about to write the chapter of my dissertation that focused on Olds's poetry. From that position, I couldn't help but imagine that in a way, I was Olds's student, and she was my instructor. I had misread her poem, and she was correcting me. I interpreted the letter and the poem as gestures toward educating me in how to read. In the letter, she warns me against reading too literally. In altering the poem, she tries to help me see the distinctions between literal and figurative language. The lesson she provides in the revised poem is that incest is a trope in the poem and not an event. The lines of the original poem read:

> And what if God had been watching when my mother
> came into my bed? What would he have done when her
> long adult body rolled on me like a
> tongue of lava from the top of the mountain and the
> tears jumped from her ducts like hot rocks and my
> bed shook with the tremors of the magma and the
> deep cracking of my nature across—

Compare these lines to those in the revised version:

> And what if God had been watching, when my mother
> came into my room, at night, to lie down on me
> and pray and cry? What did he do when her
> long adult body rolled on me
> like lava from the top of the mountain

and the magma popped from her ducts, and my bed
shook from the tremors, the cracking of my nature
across?

The words "came into my bed" in the first poem are clarified by the explanation "came into my room, at night, to lie down on me and pray and cry" in the second. This revision moves the focus from the bed to the larger room, and it clarifies the mother's actions; she was lying on her daughter, praying and crying. The simile comparing the mother's "long adult body" to a "tongue of lava" in the first version becomes simply "like lava" in the second. Olds removes the word "tongue" and so takes the focus off the bodies and places it on the simile, a figure of speech, which calls attention to the dissimilarity of two things: not lava, but like lava. And she changes "the tears jumped from her ducts" in the first version to "the magma popped from her ducts" in the second. So the bodily imagery—tongue and tears—which mingles with volcanic imagery in the first version—lava and magma—is removed. In the second version, the mother's visit is like the eruption of a volcano, and no body parts or secretions appear.

There is also a tense change from the conditional to the past: "What would he have done" versus "what did he do?" This change calls attention to the fact that the speaker of the second poem is explicitly framing a memory rather than simply remembering. But perhaps most significant is Olds's removal of the line, three-quarters of the way through the poem, "while she pried my thighs wide in the starry dark." She replaces it with "while she pried my spirit / open in the starry dark." This revision again moves the emphasis from body to nonbody. Clearly, an invasion is taking place as the speaker lies "open," but the speaker shows that it is a spiritual invasion rather than a physical one—a rape or theft of the soul.

In her letter and alterations of the original poem, Olds played the part of the well-intentioned instructor, who teaches her student (me) how to become a less-naïve, more-nuanced reader. And yet, as the figurative student in this story, I remained skeptical, though silent about my skepticism, for I did not respond to Olds's letter. I, unlike

Olds, had heard many people interpret "What If God" as a poem about incest. Indeed, I had never heard it read differently. So, to my mind, Olds represented an instructor who has a correct reading in mind, the sort of instructor who cannot tolerate readings different from her own. As a reality check, I asked a number of my colleagues what they thought was the poem's dramatic situation. Some agreed with me, others with Olds. But we all agreed that it was unusual for a poet to respond so directly to a reading of her work, and we talked about the fact that a poet is very rarely with us when we read a poem. In her gesture to clarify the poem for me, Olds crafted a less interesting, more literal poem.

About six months later, I received a second letter from Sharon Olds. She was rewriting the poem again (the poem is published in subsequent editions of *The Gold Cell*), and she wanted to thank me for "awakening [her] to a reading of [her] work that it turns out many others had made." She said that she had been "naïve, unconscious, whatever not to have realized how possible [she] had made such a reading." Most interesting in terms of the student-teacher dynamic I have been pursuing through this story, she enclosed a new poem, "To a Reader Who Wrote to Me, 'I, Too, Was an Incest Survivor,'" which she said was preinspired by her visit to Boston College.

The way that the speaker in this poem imagines the relationship of a writer to a reader revises the poet-reader:teacher-student relationship that I felt implicit in Olds's initial letter to me. In that letter, Olds, the poet, politely accused me of misreading. But in this poem, the speaker, who I would say is a poet, apologizes to a reader whose reading is fully justified:

> I am sorry I thought I could say that my mother
> pried my thighs apart and think you would
> know that it was the thighs of my soul
> she pried apart . . .

The reason the speaker apologizes, she says, is that she presumed that her reader thought like her—"I am sorry I thought I could say . . . and think you would know." Toward the end of the poem she explains why she thought this way: "I did not know, then, that there were parents who pried their children's thighs apart." The speaker apologizes for believing that what she knew of the world matched what her audience knew. She draws attention to the limitations of her own knowledge and to the power of her reader's different knowledge to challenge her assumptions.

After the speaker apologizes for assuming that her reader's experiences were like her own, she describes what her experience was. As if she were the speaker of "What If God," she tells the reader: "When she lay on me / and prayed, my pelvis ached with loneliness." This description differentiates between the bodies of speaker and reader: "here is what I felt in my pelvis," the speaker tells her reader. And I think she implies, "that is probably quite different from what you may have felt in your pelvis." By particularizing her experience, Olds's speaker makes us aware of the ways that experiences shape interpretations, that experiential differences lead to differing interpretations. But even as she shows her difference from her reader, the speaker figuratively links the incest survivor's childhood experiences to her own. She produces a chain of perpetrators and victims, those who forget and those who are forgotten:

> I forgot you, as your mother forgot you,
> as my mother forgot me, and her mother forgot her,
> and now I remember you.

This lineage, which includes the speaker herself as victim and oppressor, illustrates the speaker's recognition that imbalances of power make the dynamics of communication very complex. Both speaker and the reader who wrote are part of a long chain of people who have misread each other, each assuming that her view of the world matches that of the other. When the speaker extends her hand, she attempts to break that chain. She makes a connection across a gap in understanding.

At the end of "To a Reader Who Wrote to Me, 'I, Too, Was an Incest Survivor,'" the speaker offers a "hand / if you will take it." In our most challenging classroom situations, we can recognize the blindness of our own certainty and offer such a hand. But we must search for ways to do this which do not further prey on our students' fears and insecurities. Olds's revision process offers a model of what I have in previous chapters drawn from infant research and called "disruption and repair." In three years as an affiliate scholar at the Boston Psychoanalytic Institute, I had opportunities to witness processes of disruption and repair in the classroom from the perspective of a student, rather than a teacher. Placed in this position, I was fortunate to experience what is so easy to forget once we become the teacher: how it is that an educator who is committed to sharing authority in the classroom can, despite the most diligent efforts to do something different, become an autocratic educator.

Until I sat in a classroom at the psychoanalytic institute, I had experienced the dilemmas and pleasures of sharing authority in the classroom only from the perspective of a writing teacher, a writing program director, and a teacher of teachers. When I began to experience what it was like to be a student in a problem-posing classroom from another discipline, a discipline in which instruction in process is at least as important as instruction in content, I encountered what many students and teachers I've worked with over the years have described—the exhilaration and frustration of an educational world in which absolute truth and absolute authority no longer exist as truths but as ideas to be explored and interrogated.

Psychoanalytic educators today, like the teachers I have been describing throughout this book, struggle to maintain respect for and make use of their students' various kinds of expertise while offering instruction in the subject. No matter the field, today's educators teach in the wake of various challenges to authority and knowledge from across the disciplines in recent decades. In conversations about the clinical setting, theorists have challenged the analyst's ability to be an impartial or objective observer of the patient, emphasizing instead the mutually reciprocal influence of patient and therapist. These discussions include attention to the ways in which the analyst's experiences and theories influence the direction of the treatment. For those who are concerned about psychoanalytic teaching and learning, this work has led to a proliferation of strategies designed to invite students to assume authoritative positions in classrooms and to act as makers of knowledge in concert with their teachers.

Paulo Freire might describe this as the "problem-posing" model of education. For a problem-posing educator, "the teacher is no longer the one who teaches, but one who is himself taught in dialogue with the students, who in turn while being taught also teach" (354). Rather than depositing information into students' heads in a "banking concept" model of education, Freire suggests that, through what he calls a "problem-posing model of education," teachers and students together determine what we come to call a class. When I first enrolled in courses at the psychoanalytic institute, I was particularly struck by the problem-posing methods in a technique seminar, one based on questions, open-ended inquiry, and respect for candidates' expertise. But I was not surprised, given my own struggles to maintain problem-posing methods in the classroom, when one of the two teachers in this seminar assumed the position of the privileged knower that he was clearly trying to avoid in his classroom. When an educator assumes such a position, he recognizes neither the expertise of his students nor the spirit of open inquiry that is his pedagogical goal. But like Olds in her letters and "To a Reader Who Wrote to Me," this educator was able to recognize that he had assumed the position of objectivity in the classroom—that he had closed down the possibilities for open discussion—and to figure out (with and in front of his students) what to do next.

From the start, the two instructors in the course practiced and encouraged awareness of the relationships between the students' various kinds of expertise and the theoretical concepts we were studying as essential to the understanding of technique. The instructors regularly offered material from their own cases for the class to interpret; students and instructors were invited to act as experts together. A number of classes included reflections by one or both of the instructors on experiences with patients earlier that week, or updates on an interaction that had been discussed previously.

It was because of the democratic and challenging atmosphere in the classroom that I have just discussed, I believe, that an unusual event occurred. After about three sessions, we began to discuss our past and present experiences in the classroom—including the process of class sessions—as relevant to the issues in technique that we were exploring. Students and teachers raised issues about what someone had said in a previous session, referred to an article or a patient presented in previous weeks, or made reference to a concept they had discussed in a certain way in a past session. The students offered spontaneous examples from their own sessions with patients, and patients indirectly entered the discussion, which now included a number of different texts from different contexts.

When the students began to address what was going on between them in the here and now in terms of what they were learning together, I became fascinated by this aspect of the course; I had never seen this form of instruction discussed in either the pedagogical or psychoanalytic literature I'd read. In fact, whenever I described it to colleagues who are teachers of teachers, they found it a remarkable and exciting idea to reflect on the process of interactions in the classroom as a way to teach teachers to think about their technique. As an educator, I interpreted this aspect of the course as evidence of the problem-posing method of teaching in practice from moment to moment in the classroom. I also was reminded that this highly self-reflective method of instruction involves as many risks as it does rewards.

The sessions in the technique class I have been describing became increasingly challenging about halfway through the course, when members of the class saw fit to question the participation of both instructors and students in a particularly volatile discussion that had taken place in the third class session. As they processed their interactions in the fourth class session, the instructors and students foregrounded and then reorganized their styles of relating to each other in class discussion. This problem-posing moment in the classroom was precipitated by a perception that one instructor had adopted a tone of certainty about a student's contribution to the discussion, was joined by other students as he did so, and thereby called into question the student's interpretation of psychoanalytic technique. After some thought and consultation with other class members, the silenced student decided to address the entire seminar about it in the following class session.

I asked the members of the class (including the instructors) to read my version of the vignette that I am about to present. They provided feedback, and I revised in response. This experience emphasized for me that every reading of these two classes is itself an act of interpretation. I am interested less in the fact that something went wrong or was disrupted in this class than in how instructors and students "repaired" the group process, and even improved it, in response. They negotiated new ways of understanding the course material and each other from this experience, and *this experience* of what I would call "questioning authority" became a model for them of what it might mean to practice technique in a therapeutic context.

I am borrowing the concepts of "moments of interaction" and "disruption and repair" from an article titled "Non-Interpretive Mechanisms in Psychoanalytic Theory: The 'Something More' Than Interpretation." Here, Daniel Stern and his coauthors address the production of knowledge in psychodynamic therapy, but I find their concepts enormously useful for thinking about the production of knowledge in classrooms like the one I am trying to describe. The authors distinguish between two kinds of knowledge, "one is explicit (declarative) and the other is implicit (procedural)" (904). The first kind, explicit knowledge, would, I think, include the "facts" I just offered about the technique classroom: the texts to be read, the topics to be discussed, and the case material offered. Far from neutral or objective, all these "facts come with a point of view" (Cooper, "Facts" 255). The organization of the syllabus, the choice of articles to be discussed, the decisions about what sorts of case material to be presented and by whom—these are all forms of declarative knowledge.

The second kind of knowledge, procedural, includes "knowing about interpersonal and intersubjective relations, i.e., how 'to be with' someone"; Stern and his coauthors call this "implicit relational knowing" (905). This kind of knowledge would include the ways that students and teachers interact in classrooms, ways, I believe, that are rarely, if ever, discussed in psychoanalytic literature. In the story I am about to tell, students and instructors entered into a dialogue about this form of knowledge, even as they continued to construct ways of being together. In other words, they reflected on and continued to shape their classroom interactions by focusing on them as an object of study. This manner of thinking about the learning process seems to me to be essential to the production of knowledge in problem-posing classrooms. If the content of a course focuses on mutuality in the patient/analyst dyad, for example, shouldn't the process of the class be similarly organized around students and teachers creating knowledge in dialogue together? And how can teachers and students do this without making this process a topic for discussion in the course? In the classroom I am describing, it was.

Session One

The topic for the session I would like to focus on was "interpretation,"and the class read three articles to prepare for it: Anton Kris's "Interpretation and the Method of Free Association," Fred Busch's "In the Neighborhood: Aspects of a Good Interpretation and a Developmental Lag in Ego Psychology," and the Stern et al. article I just cited. The class began when a candidate I will call "Mike" spontaneously offered a clinical example from a session earlier in the day. Mike had seen a new patient for the second time. She told him that he reminded her of Mr. Rogers. "Tell me about Mr. Rogers," Mike said to the patient. The patient talked about her associations to Mr. Rogers, which were to playing sports. There are two kinds of players, she said. Some are hard hitting. Others just play for fun. She said she liked the ones who play for fun. "Like the mailman on Mr. Rogers," the patient said. "Mr. McFeeley!" exclaimed Mike. Both the patient and Mike laughed. Mike provided background, including that in the previous session, the patient had revealed that she was bisexual.

One of the teachers, whom I will call "Instructor A," said "she was flirting with you." One student said she was not sure why it had to be flirting. The other teacher, "Instructor B," said "she was being aggressive. Mr. Rogers is a wimp." Several students shook their heads; others nodded. One replied that she thought that many people had maternal associations to Mr. Rogers. We began to discuss our interpretations of Mr. Rogers. The class was wrestling with whether the patient was being aggressive as they explored their own associations to Mr. Rogers. Instructor B brought up the day's reading, Busch's "In the Neighborhood," in relation to the question about how to interpret the patient's analogy. What did it mean to be "in the neighborhood" in this case, he wondered? Whose neighborhood was the class talking about?

The class proceeded from a discussion of who Mr. Rogers is, to what the patient was trying to say to her analyst when she made the distinction between rough play and playing for fun, to whether Mike's response to her really addressed what she was trying to evoke in him, to what was actually represented in the reading by Busch. In this fast-paced conversation about the patient's message to her analyst, one of the students in the seminar, whom I will call "Nick," said, "Let's just say, for the sake of argument, that we say to the patient, 'you are being hostile.'" A couple of people in the class laughed, as if this were a ridiculous statement to make to a patient. It was implied in the tone of the laughter, I think, that Nick was not aware of the consequences of such an interpretation, that he was naïve or even unconscious not to have realized the damaging effects of such an accusation. (Tone, as we know, is very hard to describe, but it is an essential aspect of the implicit relationships in any classroom.)

During the next half hour, as the class continued its inquiry into whether the patient's comment could be interpreted as aggressive, Nick somehow came to represent the position of the aggressive reader in the room. At one point, Instructor B, who had initially interpreted the patient's analogy as aggressive, turned to Nick and jokingly suggested that he was the kind of analyst who would confront a patient and "tell it like it is." The accusation was repeated twice, and at least one of Nick's other classmates participated. When Nick's corner of the seminar table was gestured toward in relation to addressing a patient's hostile feelings, it became clear that Nick was having a strong reaction. He indicated his discontent by miming that he was being crucified by the class. Nobody took up his gesture for discussion, and it appeared that all assumed they were sharing a joke together.

After the class, Instructor B approached Nick and asked "if the play about his technique was okay." Nick said yes and that he took it as a sign of collegiality. But at least three of the seminar members worried that Nick was not really feeling okay about the way the class had proceeded. They separately called him that evening to discuss the situation. All three felt that the class had perhaps become over-stimulated in its discussion and that, in the midst of it, Nick came to symbolize a position rather than a person with many ways of think-ing about the issues. As one of the students who called Nick, I voiced my concern that my own playfulness in the classroom might have been unconsciously identified with Instructor's B's playfulness. His style as a teacher reminded me of my own, I told Nick, and I was wor-ried that I might have acted in concert with the instructor at Nick's expense. In any case, I was concerned that the balance of authority in the classroom had felt unduly tipped against Nick.

After he had thought about it some more, Nick decided that he was not settled about what had taken place in class, and he decided to raise the topic in the next class. He discussed his decision in advance with the classmates who had called him, and we supported him. I think it is important to note here that this student and his classmates felt com-fortable to bring an out-of-class discussion back into the classroom. It suggests to me that the dynamics in the classroom supported such a move; these students felt that it was their classroom as well as their teachers'. Although this dynamic may appear to be business as usual, my experience has suggested that such a direct challenge to an instruc-tor's authority is actually quite rare in any classroom. It is especially unusual to have students speak to each other about the process of the class and then decide to bring it to the attention of their instructors. Richard Miller reminds us of how rare this is when he remarks that "the place of unsolicited oppositional discourse [in the classroom] is no place at all" ("Fault Lines" 390).

Session Two

The following class (the topic "resistance analysis") began with Nick asking if the class could discuss the process in the previous session. He said that, in retrospect, he felt uncomfortable with how he had been responded to in the class. The air in the classroom was unusually tense. Instructor B said, "Let's talk about this. Maybe we could think about the role of aggression in our process last week?" Some seminar members said they felt that the class had had an edge to it, and several suggested that they had participated in creating that feeling.

Instructor A said that he agreed; moreover, he believed that this tone had been a part of the group's process since the term began. Instructor A suggested that the class even seemed to be evading and resisting its own aggression in some of the ways in which we talked about the texts we were reading. Both instructors waited for a moment for someone else to speak. Then Instructor B noted that more attention could be paid to the role of aggression as an everyday part of every interaction, including group process in classrooms. He pointed out that this might relate to one of the readings for the day on "resistance." It seemed as if Instructor B was ready to move on.

Nick asked if the class could wait before turning to the reading. He said that he felt that the class was not adequately responding to what had happened the previous week. The members of the seminar contributed more of their experiences of the previous discussion. I remarked that it was interesting that Instructor A's interpretation of the patient's comment about Mr. Rogers as flirtatious had completely fallen away once the aggressive reading became the topic of discussion. I thought to myself that it was easier for me to speak at this moment because I was, after all, a visitor in this room and not a candidate who would be evaluated. In addition, I was a teacher whose interpretations of technique in the previous sessions were often voiced in relation to behavior I had observed in the classrooms of the teachers I supervised. In some ways, I held the position of a different kind of authority in the room, as an individual with a Ph.D. in literature rather than an M.D., a Ph.D. in psychology, or an M.S.W.

Nonetheless, I was not the last person to speak. My classmates next discussed how it had happened that aggression, both in interpreting the patient and in the style of discussion, had become such a focus the previous week. What might the conversation have been like if they had pursued the idea that the patient was flirting with the analyst, rather than voicing aggression toward him? Why hadn't they? And was this dynamic related to the uncharacteristic silence in the previous class of Instructor A, who had suggested this reading of the situation?

Together, the class developed a thought about the place of aggression in class the previous week. Had the class become uncomfortable with its aggression and, as a way to manage it, chosen Nick as a scapegoat? When Nick offered a hypothetical question about hostility, in other words, the class became organized around him as the hostile figure: his ideas became identified with him. Instructor B and the class reacted to Nick's comment in just the way that some members of the class had suggested Nick's comment would affect the patient. In short, the group was in parallel process to the content of its session. This is what Instructor A had in mind when he said that aggression had been a part of the process of the class session. Thus at least three levels of unrecognized aggression existed in this class: toward Mike's patient, who might have been wounded by Nick's comment; toward Nick, who was scapegoated by his classmates and teacher; and toward the theorist with whom many in the class had disagreements.

Instructor B added another level of reflection to the group process. He volunteered that perhaps the class was responding to his personal style; he had in the past been experienced as blunt or too forthright in a classroom. I volunteered that I might have a too-blunt style of participating in discussion; I disagreed that it was only Instructor B's affect that had directed the conversation. After some more discussion and after Instructor B asked Nick and the class if they felt the issue had been fully discussed, the conversation moved easily to the topic for the day's session.

I think there are many ways of understanding these two class sessions, just as there are many ways of understanding what the patient may have been trying to convey to her analyst when she compared him to Mr. Rogers. But I wish to illuminate what the interactions in and outside this classroom suggest about questions of authority in teaching and learning. With regard to the classroom situation, we could say that when Nick was targeted as the aggressive reader, he became the figurative student of both the other students and his instructor. The other students joined Instructor B and became "banking concept educators" who viewed Nick as an inept and naïve reader of the patient being discussed. Despite his years of clinical experience and training in psychiatry, Nick was cast as a simplistic individual who had much to learn about practicing psychoanalysis, a novice who did not have his facts straight.

In session two, when Nick expressed his frustration at having been misinterpreted, he asked for a different understanding of his role in the discussion and in the classroom itself. Nick became a problem-posing educator, urging his classmates and teachers to rethink their relationships to each other and, simultaneously, to consider the knowledge that they were constructing. Nick's insistence on further talk about his experiences in the classroom the previous week also drew the attention of class members to their creation of knowledge together; if even one of the six members of the class felt driven out of the conversation, the entire group would have a relationship to the topics they were pursuing different from that which had occurred during the previous session.

Nick's comments in the second session also offered an important and specific lesson about instructors who teach psychoanalysis. His insistence that the class revisit the previous week's conversation in some detail called attention to blindnesses in the original discussion, blindnesses that were in part produced by Instructor B's tone of absolute certainty. In the power relations in a classroom, Nick was a student in the class, no matter how much it felt like a democratic and open atmosphere. Given this power dynamic, it was a risk for him to ask the class to consider its process the previous week. Nick was raising the class's awareness to the fact that any instructor's opinion, when voiced in a classroom, carries more weight than that of any student, regardless of the situation. When instructors speak, they carry the institutional authority of the teacher, the authority inherent in the role. Although instructors cannot escape that fact, they can consider how they make use of that authority, especially when they use the authority in ways that obfuscate the authority and expertise of others in the classroom.

Nick might never have raised the issue if the instructors in this seminar were not vigilantly aware of their uses of authority in the classroom. The hierarchical order of a traditional classroom does not shape the interactions in this classroom. Instead, there is a give-and-take in which both the instructor and the student assume positions of authority in the conversation and in which both instructor and student cause the class to focus on how their personal histories shape their interactions there. It is therefore a classroom in which what Edward Tronick defines as "co-creation" figures prominently; students and teachers participate in shaping what they call a class. Deborah Britzman explains that "both the desire for love and the anxiety of losing love are brought into the classroom. . . . [S]tudents enact earlier conflicts as they vie for the teacher's love" ("Between 'Lifting'" 6–7). The case that I am exploring raises the possibility that teachers also vie for love in the classroom, although in most cases their "conflicts" are harder to see.

What if Nick had taken the more typical position of silence when he felt injured by what had happened in his class? What if he had deemed his teachers' love more important than his own experiences and emotional responses? In that case, his experience may well have been invalidated or even unnoticed, even by himself. In the words of linguist Mary Louise Pratt, "If a classroom is analyzed as a social world unified and homogenized with respect to the teacher, whatever students do other than what the teacher specifies is invisible to the analysis" (14). Nick's supposedly naïve interpretation of the patient's situation would have been "invisible" to the class's "analysis" if Nick had not raised the issue in the following class session.

If we think about this vignette in relation to Stern and his coauthors' concept of "implicit relational knowledge," it adds another level of understanding to what happened. Both the instructors and students were learning other ways for teachers and students to be with one another than banking concept models of teacher-student relationships allow. Paulo Freire notes that in such a model of education, "the teacher confuses the authority of knowledge with his or her own professional authority" (350). Freire refers to the ways that an instructor's ideas can become the truths, or even the gods, in his classroom. Irwin Hoffman talks about a similar phenomenon in psychoanalysis, when he argues that "the whole ritual of psychoanalysis is designed, in part, to cultivate and protect a certain aura or mystique that accompanies the role of the analyst" (151–52). Freire and Hoffman might have similar ways of understanding the mystique of the senior analyst as truthsayer in the psychoanalytic classroom. The classroom I described, with its atmosphere of mutuality, disruption, frank discussion, and repair, contrasts with this idealization. The Stern et al. article would suggest that the interaction I described contained "special 'moments' of authentic person-to-person connection . . . that altered the relationship [in this case, between the teachers and the students] in this classroom" (Stern et al. 906).

Educational theorists such as Kurt Spellmeyer warn that an educator's beliefs about the knowledge she has to impart do not necessarily correspond in any direct way to her uses of authority. Although an instructor believes that knowledge is context driven, that is, dependent on the knower and historically situated, the instructor may remain entrenched in ideas about what is good for the students. In fact, Spellmeyer believes that teaching practices have actually not changed much at all, despite the recent focus on situated knowledges and shared authority in the classroom, stating that "the theoretical debate about what to teach and how to teach it has not fundamentally changed teaching as a social practice—or rather, as a practice of socialization largely designed to reproduce our values and advance our objectives" ("After Theory" 901). Spellmeyer expresses concern that deeply held ideas about what is "correct" continue to shape the pedagogical decisions of even the most "progressive" instructors.

Deborah Britzman adds a cautionary note from the realm of group education when she identifies "a reticence to investigate the difficulties groups have in making and encountering knowledge that allows individuals new experiments in working creatively and ethically with each other" ("Thoughts" 332). Norman Holland and Murray Schwartz anticipated these difficulties decades ago, when they spoke of the need for teachers who combine "the inner experience of therapy or analysis with the theoretical study of a discipline" (792). The class that I have described might constitute just such an experiment, in which questions about teachers' attempts at "objectivity" in the classroom were in play (Holland 336).

People in a classroom work to create safety and take risks together, and the instructors lead the way. When instructors discover through their students, as Instructor B did, that they have somehow disregarded or closed down the possibilities for creative exploration in the room, I believe their primary responsibility is to call attention to it and decide, with their students, what to do next. Because a brave student took a risk that was supported by his instructors and colleagues, the class I described entered a more fruitful, open, and risk-taking environment. It is a model for what we might accomplish in any classroom in which the authority of our students is of primary importance.

In my experience as an authority in the classroom, I have observed that difficult moments offer me opportunities to identify my own theories, or versions of the truth, as they are reflected back to me in my students' responses. The next step of the dialogue can be lost if I wrongly locate the source of misunderstanding or difficulty in the student's passivity or unpreparedness or ascribe it to "a bad day." If I can bear to look at myself through the lenses my students provide at these moments, I believe that they can serve as interpreters of my own behavior of which I am unaware, as well as of the ways in which I can become deaf to my students' ideas in the service of my own.

Consider this comment, from an award-winning teacher at an institution that enrolls students with very high grades and SAT scores: "When they are not talking, and I have tried every kind of question I know, I simply throw up my hands and lecture; this can go on for a semester. So I just chalk up the bad classes to experience and wait for the next good one to come along." For this teacher, there is nothing to be done about students who do not answer her pointed textual questions. When her usual moves do not work, the class enters a stalemate, which she ends by becoming the only speaker in the room. We might argue that this teacher needs discussion-leading strategies to help her save the bad class. I might agree, except that when I have offered teachers I supervise a set of suggestions, the teachers often found their discussions still lacking in energy and direction. I have also tried those techniques myself, with mixed results. These experiences have led me to believe that more than a set of discussion-leading skills is needed to improve our discussions. We need ways of thinking that are more specific to particular groups of students, and these ways of thinking will inevitably lead us back to our own participation in making the class what it is or is not. We will be able to discover that participation, however, only if we attend to what our students' disagreeable behaviors elicit in us.

Even when we are not "pretending" to know the truth, our personal experiences and beliefs are "enshrined in [our] theories" (Stolorow and Atwood 356). Through careful attention to others' reactions to us, our private theories become accessible for reflection. In what I have described above, a poet and an instructor identified the mythologies of their reading and teaching practices as they heard them back through others. Any teacher's ability to hear rests on his or her willingness to recognize that a classroom is not one but many neighborhoods and that we and our students inhabit many neighborhoods at once. When we assume that we know which one we are talking about, we are in danger of leaving somebody outside the gate.

Is there a perfect classroom? If we consider Wallace Stevens's poem in light of the stories I told above, our goal might better be to embrace the "imperfect paradise" of the "never-resting mind." Through the constant interplay of disruption and repair, we can embrace Stevens's challenge to transform the inevitably "bitter" misunderstandings in the classroom into "delight."

CHAPTER SIX

SHOULD THE TEACHER BE THE TEXT?
Self-Revelation in the Classroom

Intelligence is all about knowing the right
story to tell at the right time.
—Roger C. Schank and John E. Cleave,
"Natural Learning, Natural Teaching"

ALTHOUGH MUCH OF WHAT WE KNOW AS TEACHERS IS INVISIBLE
to us because of the teacher's location as the authority in the classroom, some of our most meaningful interactions with students come
when we choose to reveal ourselves as human beings. We tell stories
about things that have happened to us, offer details about our personal lives, or provide opinions about topics the class is discussing.
Talking about our own lives in the classroom can lead to moments of
authentic connection to our students, moments when the class consists no longer of students and teachers inhabiting their roles but of
a group of human beings working together toward understanding. It

is always possible, however, that our stories will be interpreted as obsequious quests for students' approval or narcissistic interjections in which we become the text in the class. When we bring ourselves into the classroom, especially when we are new to teaching, we must be mindful of what we are trying to accomplish. We want to show that we are not faceless voices of the institution but passionate human beings who have deep attachments to our students and the subject. But we also need to be aware that we are in the classroom to teach, not to burden students with our personal lives.

How can we discuss details of our personal lives with our students without becoming the text in the class? Should we, for example, come out as gay or even straight to our students? Should we tell them whether we identify ourselves as feminist? Moslem? Christian? Atheist? Conservative? Liberal? Athletic? World-traveled? Published? Should we frown on articulations of racism, classism, homophobia, or sexism in class discussions? Should we express our distress about the government's response to September 11? Should we chronicle our third grader's efforts to learn to write complete paragraphs?

My friend Henry would say most emphatically that we should not. Henry tells his students barely anything about himself until very late in the term, if ever. He does not confess his love for Gertrude Stein and Wallace Stevens. He does not say that he was a union organizer before he became a writing teacher. He does not mention that he is gay, although his dress and accessories, including a gay rights pin, would suggest that he is. For Henry, it is important that students have room to experiment with many ideas about him, including his sexuality. This, he argues, will allow them to explore many possible ways for them to inhabit their bodies in this world.

When I first taught a literature course, I took Henry's advice. I knew him to be the most popular young teacher in our department, so I tried to model myself after him so as to manage my fear that I was not qualified to be teaching poetry to sophomores in college when I had not yet finished my dissertation. I decided not to reveal one detail of my personal life to my students. I dressed very professionally and prepared for class in as determined a fashion as I ever have.

Each day a group of students led the class in talking about a poem, offering their own close readings to the class of thirty-five. When questions arose, I answered the ones that the group leading the discussion did not know the answers to. After the group presentation, I would lead the class in discussing a second poem. Class conversations always stayed very close to the language of the poems, to the *Oxford English Dictionary*, and to the play of literal meaning and figure in the text.

One day, a student asked me a question to which I did not know the answer. "I don't know," I said. "I think we'll have to look that up unless someone can help me out here."

There was a loud sigh. The entire class seemed to be basking in a wave of relief. It occurred to me that they had the impression that I felt that I always needed to provide them with the correct answer. They did not believe that I saw myself as a flawed human being. I had become an automaton rather than a teacher in the classroom. Once I admitted that my knowledge was limited, I became a much more real and, I would argue, better teacher for them. I also opened the possibility that students could begin to experience something human in their poetry course. For me, poetry had always been a way to explore multiple and often-conflicting interpretations. It was a shock when I realized that that was hardly the impression my stiff demeanor was conveying to my students.

I was taken aback by the sigh of relief in the classroom, but I was not surprised. I knew that something was wrong in the poetry class because it did not feel meaningful to me. In refusing to provide any details about myself in the classroom, I was effectively hiding from my students. I was hiding behind my training in close reading, an *Oxford English Dictionary*, and my own interpretations of the poems. My students could literally see me in the classroom, but they could not really see me. Instead of being a human being to them, I was a robotic figure, and their readings of the poetry were somewhat robotic as well. Poetry, which for me represented the riches of human experience, had become a regimented, desolate world for my students.

To explore how to improve the atmosphere in the poetry class, I decided to observe Henry's class. It occurred to me that I was misinterpreting his reluctance to share himself with the students. I was astonished by what I saw. It was true that Henry did not directly discuss particularly intimate details of his personal life with his students. But Henry was very personal with them. He shared stories about what he had read in the newspaper, offered a narrative about a colleague from another department who was trying to figure out why students should write in college, and asked students' opinions about the big AIDS rally that had recently been held on campus. Henry's life as a gay man, a reader of Stein and Stevens, and a political activist was not literally the text in his class, nor should it have been, necessarily. But aspects of his life were still present in the classroom.

Henry's class made the issue of self-revelation in the classroom more complex for me. From their conversation about subjectivity when I was there, I gathered that Henry's students perceived that they were invited to play with identity in the classroom, to experiment with many ways of being a self, just as their teacher talked about the many ways that people in his world conceived of themselves. When I first heard him talk about keeping his personal life out of class, I had thought that Henry was a closed person in the classroom, the faceless voice of the institution, as I was in my poetry class. But my visit revealed Henry to be far warmer, more personal, and more accessible than I was in the poetry class. Henry was not hiding behind his role as I had. He cultivated a personal presence, making use of his experiences to encourage his students to connect with the subject. His version of authenticity included comments about his friends, colleagues, people on the news, and those in the corridors of the campus. They did not, however, include revelations that were strictly about his personal experiences.

Henry's decision to reveal few details of his personal life to his students was designed to protect students' developing ideas about themselves as subjects in the world so that they would have room to be complex people with multiple identities. He found a way to inhabit the role as teacher that protects himself and his students from the dangers of overexposure, a case in which the teacher's identity can become limited for the teacher and the students. If Henry were to say

"I am gay" or "I think George Bush is incompetent," he would argue, the students would not have space to imagine their teacher as straight, bisexual, Republican, or anything else. They would also not have as much liberty to imagine these identities for themselves.

In the classroom, students and teachers often relate to each other through their perceived professional roles. The roles of teacher and student can facilitate the enforcement of rules and policies that allow us to maintain boundaries and structure in the classroom, but they often trip us up when we want to become more than we feel is possible within the assigned role. When teachers feel inhibited in their personal interactions with students, they sometimes fall back on what Paulo Freire calls "banking concept" images of education. As banking concept educators, we deliver information to our students rather than making knowledge with them. We treat our students as receptacles to be filled with information, rather than complex and experienced people in their own right. A teacher's banking concept attitudes can leave students feeling empty, baffled, or even distressed.

The relationship between personal revelation and institutional roles was no more present for me than when I met with a distressed student who approached me near the end of my first semester as director of composition at Emerson College. The student said that her teacher would not allow her back into the classroom because she had missed twelve classes, and the syllabus said that she could not miss more than five. She had missed the classes because someone she had taken into her life as if he were her grandfather had died and she had gone to California for the funeral, and because she had been depressed when she got back. She demanded to know why her teacher was being so unreasonable. The student was yelling. She sounded like a victim of a terribly unjust and erratic system, a system that made no sense at all.

After explaining the policy and discussing the reasons for her absences, I said that I could not change the policy. I was sorry, but she would have to withdraw. The student said that this was the rule in other departments with other kinds of courses as well. She said that my colleagues in other departments interpreted the rule differently. I asked her which departments these were, for I was concerned that I might be misinterpreting the policy. I said that perhaps I could ask them about this. She replied, "Now you are patronizing me." I said that I was trying to understand how the student saw the situation because it was different from how I did.

"Why are you so unbending," the student demanded, at a high pitch, "when everyone at this institution knows what the rules are and no one pays attention to them?"

"I am director of composition," I told her solemnly. "I am enforcing the rules that we have in our department."

"Fine," she said, "but you were not the director last year."

"No, I was not," I said.

"Could I speak to your superior?" she asked.

I said, "Certainly," and gave her the telephone number of the chair of my department. I looked down at my desk to hide the surge of fear that was rushing through my body.

The student said, "Well, I don't want to go over your head; I just want to stay in the class."

I said I was sorry that she was having so much frustration over this, that I was certain she had not intended to miss all these classes. I offered a personal detail: I too had lost an "adopted" grandfather when I was around her age and had found it really hard and depressing. But I lost my grandfather in the summer, I told her. I commented that it must be difficult to try to concentrate when she had to go to school and grieve at the same time.

The student began to cry. To give her some privacy to compose herself, I offered to go down the hall and get her a tissue. When I returned, she talked through her tears about how frustrating this was, how her parents were going to be furious and would not understand, that it was costing them so much money, that she might not graduate on time. I sat in silence, nodding and offering sympathetic looks.

"Would you like me to speak to them?" I asked. I said I didn't think I could do anything to keep her in the class, but I would investigate, consider the situation more, and let her know the next day. When I arrived in my office the following morning, there was a message from her stating that she realized she should withdraw and was doing so. She thanked me for trying to help her and said that ours was one of the few "humane" interactions she had had at this institution.

My revelation of my own experience in this case was very helpful to the student. It gave her the dose of humanity that she had been looking for at the college. Although I was not her teacher, I was in an institutional role, and I was initially perceived as being inhibited as a person because of that role. But the student invited me to step out of institutional roles when she first threatened to talk to my chair but then said that she did not want to go over my head. She invited me to join her in another kind of interaction, a human relationship in which she had become generous and sensitive to my position as a new employee.

Not long after I had seen this student, the "unreasonable" teacher came to me, visibly flustered. She asked if the student had come by and then began defending herself to me. "The syllabus states the rule clearly," she said. "The student must be out of her mind. Does she think the rules don't apply to her?" The teacher sounded like the spokesperson for the rules, the voice of the institution. She sounded, in other words, just like I had when I first spoke to her angry student.

This teacher and I both assumed the voice of the institution in the above exchanges, I believe, because we became invested in maintaining the structure of a pedagogical world that felt precarious when we perceived our authority to be under attack. Hiding our fears in the rules, we became unable to speak to the actual student in our own voices. We each lost contact with ourselves because we were new in our positions and felt so threatened that we could only defend ourselves.

Psychodynamic theorist Joseph Sandler might use the term "role-responsiveness" to explain what happened: "The relationship between [student and teacher] is in large part (though of course, not wholly) determined by . . . the intrapsychic role-relationship which each party tries to impose on the other. . . . [W]e may see a whole variety of role-relationships emerge [in any situation]. . . . [W]hat I want to emphasize is that the role-relationship of the [student] at any particular time consists of a role in which she casts herself and a *complementary* role in which she casts the [teacher] at any particular time" (44).

Sandler might say that the student's anger originally placed her instructor and me in the role of authority figures who read the institution's rules too literally, but also that the instructor and I, each new to our respective roles as teacher and director, unconsciously emphasized that this student was in an unacceptable position in order to maintain our authority. So we might say that the student had pulled the teacher and me into the role of defender of the institution. But we might also say that we pulled the student into a defensive position in order to protect ourselves. We choose what we will say, which in part was invented by and in part invents a role for our listener, and we hear what role our listener fashions for us in response. If we can be flexible as we hear ourselves being invented, we can reinvent ourselves in response.

Our awareness of the roles we choose to play and are pulled to play can help us become more aware of how we make use of ourselves as teachers. With this knowledge, we might imagine ourselves into ways of being more the flexible, variously positioned, and discursive acrobats that Henry represents in his classroom. In the world, we know too well what it is like "to feel like one self while being many" (Bromberg 516). But how often are we able to live that in our classrooms?

As we think about what to reveal to our students about ourselves, we stretch the boundaries of our classrooms, making space for different kinds of play with our students. Donna Killian Duffy and Janet Wright Jones recognize the importance of "spaces" in *Teaching within the Rhythms of the Semester*: "The classroom environment reflects many kinds of spaces . . . and each of these spaces is open to negotiation, to manipulation, and to ownership" (40). I am most interested in moments when ownership becomes transformed into a more flexible give-and-take with another person: that is, when we can begin to play.

D. W. Winnicott explains that "playing is doing" (41). When we tell our students about ourselves for a particular reason, or with an intention, we are doing something, and we are inviting them to do something as well. But what should the teacher *do*, for example, when she is almost the same age as her students? In this case, a teacher's self-revelations can illuminate the slight difference in age and experience between teacher and student, drawing a useful line between varying levels of expertise in the room and making students feel safe to be in the presence of someone who has struggled with the same issues, but a short time ago. When I first started teaching, I was three years older than my students, and they told me that they knew this almost as soon as I met them. I had graduated with the brother of one of my students, and he was happy to tell the class this fact. Once the students knew my age, I felt that I should be honest about other things as well, such as where I lived and how I spent my weekend. I wanted to know my students as people and was very eager to be liked by them. I was also, as is obvious, far too willing to talk too openly about myself in the classroom. And I doubted that I was actually qualified for the job.

While it might also have produced a too-casual atmosphere in the classroom, especially because it underlined my discomfort, my willingness to reveal myself to my students would not necessarily have been detrimental to the class if it had been even slightly more judicious. I felt strangely ill at ease in the front of the classroom, and I was certain that the students were ill at ease as well. Their classroom roles, I surmised, bore little resemblance to who they were in the rest of their lives as new college students. I felt almost as if the comments I expressed about myself in the classroom were fictions to my students, even though they knew at least one of them, my age, to be true. Regardless of what I told them, my students did not find me real in the first place. When I added details from my personal life to an already-inauthentic image, I simply compounded their inability to reach me and did nothing for my ability to reach them. I felt powerless and exposed, rather than friendly and accessible. In this case, the personal stories I offered fell flat.

When teachers tell stories about themselves, they often are trying to step away from their roles as professionals in an academic institution and become more present to their students as themselves. This was my intention in that first class. But my stories only increased my entrenchment in a rigid version of the teacher's role. Another teacher who was perceived as nearly the same age as her students had quite the opposite experience when she made use of her personal experience to address the issue. She used the fact of her age to create a boundary rather than to break one down. This teacher shared an office with me in graduate school. She told me how she handled the fact that she looked younger than most of her students. At first she was mortified, imagining they knew that she was not qualified to teach, was immature, and had only just graduated from college. Then she realized that her students would never know how old she was, which was actually ten years older than they were, unless she somehow told them. She decided to try to find a way to reveal that she was older in order to make herself, and perhaps all of them, feel that she was qualified to teach.

In the middle of a discussion about a poem by Yeats to his daughter, the teacher raised the issue of Yeats's representation of what it means to have a daughter and whether he was somehow imagining what it meant to be a daughter as well. This was a hard one, she speculated, to speak both from the position of parent and child. "Actually," she commented, "my son would be happy to tell you that I never understand his position." The teacher looked at her book for a moment as she heard the students shuffling in their seats and glancing at each other. The atmosphere in the classroom was never as casual as it had been before her revelation, and the teacher felt the students subsequently respected her much more.

When I told this story to a new teacher at Emerson, who was also having trouble in the classroom with her age, she told me, "But I don't have a child, and I am almost the same age as my students. My students think I should come to happy hour with them on Friday night." This teacher needed to transform a potential embarrassment into a productive classroom interaction. She felt that she was losing touch with her students as students and being perceived by them as a drinking buddy. She was not distanced and flat in the classroom, as I was, and her dilemma actually sparked something in me. I believe that I was envious that she had achieved such intimacy with them, and yet I worried that she had abdicated her role as teacher at the same time.

I had a flashing vision of the teacher storming into the classroom, announcing what the rules were, and providing an image of who the students should be. If that didn't work, I thought, perhaps I could join her in class and bring more authority to the scene. I wanted the authority to come from the outside, as a kind of force. This was the absolute worst response, I remarked to myself. Subtlety and self-revelation would prove much more effective, and those were the qualities the teacher was asking for advice about in the first place.

But what could she say? I asked her if she thought that she had had experiences that the students had not had. She could not think of any. We started to talk about her experiences as a reader and writer. "What about your undergraduate experiences?" I asked. "Might you refer to a teacher you had in college and contrast her approach with how you now think about writing?" This seemed promising. She also considered discussing the summer writing workshop in Vermont in which she had participated. There she had met lots of famous writers and had learned much in conversations with them. Weaving her experiences into the conversation about reading and writing helped to instill confidence in this young teacher. She was making use of her expertise, which she had not realized she possessed, to nurture the expertise of her students. But the teacher's experience as a reader and writer is one of the "safest" ways to reveal personal details in a classroom. Much harder to gauge are the details of being human that have apparently no relationship to the course material.

The consequences of self-revelation at the wrong time or in the wrong context have become clear to me through interactions in which what I expected students to hear was not what they actually heard me saying to them. Consider a simple example from the middle of my career, when I was teaching a class of adults in the evening. A boisterous group, they had been ready to talk the minute I first walked in the door and announced that I was their teacher. They had already been discussing which of the essays in the textbook they would like to read first. Playing along with them, I asked them to choose what they would read. They chose a short story by Joyce Carol Oates, called "Marya." A Bob Dylan song frames the story. To make a connection with the students, who were already well connected to each other, I joked: "Isn't he just great? I think he might be almost as good as Springsteen." I also named a few of my favorite Dylan songs.

When I received the first papers of these wonderfully talkative students, I was baffled about what to do with a long one by a student named Karen. She had written about how she and her friend had accidentally stumbled upon Bruce Springsteen playing at the Stone Pony bar in Asbury Park one Friday night when they were in high school. The paper was a six-page narrative about the incident, which did not mention the Oates story except to say "this reminds me of . . ." I gave the paper a "not passing" and asked Karen to write another. She was devastated when she received the paper. She had apparently thought that my announcement about Bruce Springsteen offered the class a glimpse of what I wanted to hear about in student papers. She also expected that I would appreciate what a great moment she had had, since I loved Springsteen too. I told her that I did appreciate it but did not really know how to relate this appreciation to the assigned question. Quite literally, I had become the text in this student's class.

Although I felt like a playful banterer in the classroom on the first night of class, at least one of my students experienced my "gift" of information about Bruce Springsteen as a magical charm. When I was talking about Bruce Springsteen and Bob Dylan, my role as teacher was still foremost in her mind, and not nearly so in mine. Speaking about analysts and their patients, Irwin Hoffman cautions that despite the emphasis on mutuality and sharing in the analytic dyad, "there is [still] likely to be a special affirming power associated with the analyst's willingness to engage with the patient in a way that is personally expressive and spontaneous. The source of that power is precisely in the ritualized asymmetry that promotes a view of the analyst as elevated in some sense and as beyond the patient's reach. In that context the analyst's personal and emotional availability can become a kind of magical gift" (119). The asymmetrical roles of analyst and patient bear some important similarities to those between teacher and student. No matter how "mutual" we try to make the encounter, the stories we offer our students about ourselves very often feel like "magical gifts" to them.

In the early part of this century, when it was more common to see the teacher as an objective deliverer of facts to students, discussions of self-revelation were not as central as they are today. We no longer see the teacher as an objective holder of knowledge but instead as a biased participant in the educational process. This same movement has occurred in the profession of psychoanalysis, in which the analyst is for the most part no longer perceived as the representative of scientific objectivity and technical neutrality, no longer "a rational, relatively distant, neutral, anonymous scientist-observer" (Aron 21).

Psychoanalysis was once as it is depicted in Woody Allen's films or in the pages of the *New Yorker*. The analyst was conceived as a "blank screen" upon whom patients (from the couch) projected their unconscious conflicts. A nearly silent witness to a monologue, the analyst was permitted to provide only interpretations of the patient's problems and never the smallest "hints of suggestion, guidance, or opinion, that reflected aspects of [his or her] personality" (Jacobs 161). The objective interpretation, delivered in exactly the right words at exactly the right time in exactly the right tone, supposedly offered the patient the key to his or her conflicts. Although it was never fully true, the analyst was understood to be outside the frame. Owen Renik makes the important point that it is a mistake to imagine that analysts did not reveal themselves when they sat as silent blank screens behind the couch: "The question becomes not whether to disclose, but how to manage the unavoidable condition of constant disclosure" (467). Whatever we say or do not say, Renik argues, makes a statement about ourselves to the people with whom we interact.

Today it is much more common for psychoanalysts to see themselves as partners in a mutual struggle for understanding, a struggle focused on the patient but engaging the full self of each party. In short, analysts cannot even pretend to hide any more, because they exist as coparticipants in the therapeutic process: "The patient-analyst relationship [is] continually established and reestablished through ongoing mutual influence in which both patient and analyst systematically affect, and are affected by, each other" (Aron, "Clinical Choices" 23). Each analysis depends almost entirely on the two people involved and the relationship they forge together. Relational and intersubjective models of therapy cast the analyst as a more skilled interactive partner than his or her patient but rarely as the objective or godlike expert that professional analytic training was once thought to produce.

The pages of contemporary psychoanalytic journals have featured much discussion concerning how to think about what to explicitly reveal to the patient when the analyst is understood as inevitably self-revelatory, a coparticipant in the analytic process. Theodore Jacobs reminds us that decisions about self-revelation, like all decisions of the analyst, depend entirely on the context: "We must . . . adjust our approach to the material at hand. . . . [T]his means responding to patients with a directness that may include the disclosure of a piece of personal information or the sharing of a subjective experience" (172). Context and personal style, these writers suggest, mean more than what we say about ourselves.

My least successful example of deliberate self-disclosure as a teacher took place when I first taught a course in twentieth-century women's literature at Rutgers University. There were fifty students in the class, and they were eager, talkative, and ready to read almost anything I gave them. I felt as comfortable with this class as any I have taught, and my comfort led to some risk taking in the realm of self-revelation. The material also contributed to this feeling, I suspect, for much of it was written by African American women writers such as Audre Lorde, bell hooks, and Toni Morrison, for whom truth telling is exceptionally important.

At the time, I was writing my dissertation about representations of incest in twentieth-century women's poetry. My mother is an incest survivor, and I felt that I had finally found a way to explore a bit of her personal, painful history without causing her further harm by asking her to tell me more about her past than that fact. I taught two of the poems from my dissertation in the course, and in passing, I revealed to the class that my mother's history had sparked my interest in this subject. I was spurred to reveal this fact, I believe, by a quote from Audre Lorde that I read at the time, in which she meditates on this question: What are the things you do not say?

At the end of what I thought was a fabulous course, I received a letter from the therapist of one of my students in the class. The letter said that the therapist's patient (my student) had been working out childhood experiences of sexual abuse that semester and that when I told the class I was a daughter of an incest survivor, she felt overwhelmed by that information. She also felt unsafe in the class when I taught Anne Sexton's poem "Briar Rose," which represents father-daughter incest, and a poem by Stevie Smith, "Papa Loves Baby," that treats the same subject. The therapist warned me of the potentially dangerous consequences of revealing too much of my mother's traumatic history to students who might themselves be trauma survivors. The therapist asked me to reconsider the content of the poetry I taught or, at the very least, how I presented its graphic material. The letter shocked and confused me, pushing me to challenge how I taught this volatile material. It made me wonder why a therapist would see it as her job to protect her patient from the world in which incest was a reality, rather than teaching her patient to protect herself in that world. But it scared me as well and made me become much more cautious about discussing myself in the classroom.

I almost always tell graduate students about the therapist's letter concerning her patient to illustrate the complexities of my decision to reveal my mother's experience as an incest survivor. My intention at the time, I tell them, was to introduce the detail in order to reassure students who were meeting representations of incest in poetry. I wanted students to know that incest was a fact of life, that it was common, that incest survivors write poetry, and that they are also mothers. But I did not consider the consequences of introducing a topic in the room against which any number of students were already defended. Judith Harris might have suggested that before I spoke about this topic I "weigh the benefits of uninformed commentary against an already informed silence" (*Signifying Pain* 194).

My classroom commentary about representations of incest was informed by reading Michel Foucault, who argues that because speech about topics like incest is culturally silenced, those who speak about it risk being interpreted rather than heard, and their utterances reach the status of confession: "the obligation to confess is now relayed through so many different points, is so deeply ingrained in us, that we no longer perceive it as the effect of a power that constrains us; on the contrary, it seems to us that truth, lodged in our most secret nature, 'demands' only to surface; that if it fails to do so, this is because a constraint holds it in place . . . and it can finally be articulated only at the price of a kind of liberation" (60). The students in my literature class might have become uncomfortable by my revelations about incest because they were called upon to act as interpreters, while I was aligning myself with a victim, my mother, and so pulling for them to assume the more powerful position as I remained with the survivors and the poets. The classroom could become bifurcated around this dichotomy of interpreter and victim, I have told the graduate students, which is something I would consciously work against if I were to teach such poetry again.

When I first shared this anecdote in a graduate course, I was very nervous. I was afraid that I would offend another survivor. But I was also sure that something like this could happen to one of these teachers, and I wanted us to explore my mistake. After class I received a voice mail from a student. She sounded like she was crying. Here is what she said: "As I sat in the foreign world of the graduate composition class, afraid that I was once again not qualified to be in a place, I suddenly heard words that were familiar to me. When you shared with the class a story from your teaching career that raised the issue of how much any teacher should share with her class, you seemed to be speaking directly to me. Embedded in your story were the words, 'I am the daughter of a sexual abuse survivor.' I had never heard anyone say that aloud before, least of all me. Although I already had great respect for you as my teacher and a lover of teaching, I was amazed that we shared this bond, that there are other daughters like me in the world, and that rather than locating myself in the shame and silence that was my mother's experience, I can find myself in our classroom. I suddenly felt that there was actually room for me in this academic world, that I am not an impostor. Your willingness to be so open about something so painful teaches me that my experience also has a place in the world and that I am not alone. What I feel right now is relief, and I would like to thank you for that. It is not something I am used to feeling."

It is somewhat embarrassing for me to present this student's message, for it feels as if I am trying to exonerate myself and blow my own horn at the same time. Yet this experience convinced me that self-revelation, like any other utterance in the classroom, can be understood by students in innumerable ways. This is the risk that we choose to take in the classroom, and I would argue that it is worth taking.

The letter from the cautious therapist and my students' audible sighs when I finally said that I did not know something in the poetry class mark extremes of my experiences with self-revelation in the classroom. Working between these extremes over the years, I have learned that students need me to be vulnerable but not needy, authentic but not obsequious in the classroom. I have also learned that students do not always interpret my self-revelations in the ways that I imagine. My thoughts about self-revelation have been complicated by conversations with colleagues and new instructors, particularly those in which we have struggled with how to approach those things that may be obvious about ourselves in the classroom—that we are orthodox Jews, lesbians, African Americans, or survivors of polio, for example. Should we draw attention to these realities or allow our students to play with the possibilities that they might present for the students if they are not named or defined in a particular way?

These questions have plagued me throughout my career as a teacher, for I have always wanted my classes to feel like the best ones I have had—lessons in life as well as in the subject. I share many of these life lessons when discussing boundary issues in the graduate-level Teaching of Composition course. I want the students to know how much of learning how to teach is about getting it wrong, being misunderstood, or feeling frustrated when the class does not go as we imagined it would.

Here is a story I always tell them near the end of the course, and it is one I am happy to offer at the end of this book. It was my first official full-time teaching job and the first time I was director of a writing program. But it was not the first time I was trying to teach while depressed. I remember sitting in my spacious office, surrounded by my books, a Native American rug I'd found at a yard sale, and two comfy chairs I'd discovered in the office supply room. I remember looking at the door when I walked in. It said "Dawn Skorczewski. Director of Composition." Outside it was Southern California: hot, sunny, tropical. Palm trees swayed in the breeze. Inside, the shades had been drawn to protect my eyes. My head was on my arms. How was I going to teach Virginia Woolf when I could not focus on the text?

I summoned up the only story that would help me get through the following seventy-five minutes. I told myself that during class, the San Andreas fault was finally going to give way, and the class, the building, everything would be demolished. We would not survive. So the next hour would be my last on this planet, it would be with these students, and we would be talking about *To the Lighthouse*. How would I make that a meaningful experience for all of us? This would be my challenge. During class, we talked about whether Mrs. Ramsey and Lily ever found hope in their world. What evidence could we find of hope in the text? An hour and a half later, as I left the classroom, I realized that I had almost forgotten about my depression. I felt that I had changed from my earlier self: I was now proud of myself as a teacher and as a person. Teaching, as usual, was saving my life.

Whenever I tell this story to students in the Teaching of Composition course, they laugh. It is so dramatic and unconvincing to them. They do not feel the depression that I felt, in the way that I felt it, because it is not theirs and because I deliberately tell the story in a way that will elicit their laughter at my expense. But I do not tell the story only to make them laugh. I tell it so that they will be reminded that what is on the surface is often not all that is going on in a person, especially when the person performs a public role such as teacher. And I tell the story to raise the question of how much we should say about ourselves directly in a classroom, and what effect our statements about ourselves have on our students. I remind the students that I may be telling them too much about my struggles in the past, that I cannot be sure, and that I cannot ask them directly about it because how could they honestly respond and still feel safe in a classroom in which I am the teacher? But I also tell them that I offer that particular painful story to raise as many questions as we can about the benefits and risks of self-revelation in the classroom.

In personal correspondence, Peter Elbow points out that one of the biggest obstacles to self-revelation in the classroom is fear of how we will be perceived by our students: "Should I tell things about me that will make many of my students look down on me or scorn me or be threatened or even disgusted by me?" We can never be sure about the answer to this question, but we can be certain that what one student experiences will not be the same as what another does. Elbow points out that "this issue becomes heightened when teachers may be more easily threatened by students (because they are new, racially marked, physically small, female)." We take risks when we tell stories about ourselves to our students; however, as I have tried to establish throughout this book, we almost always take risks when we attempt to engage in authentic relationships in the classroom.

Ursula Kelly suggests that "we ask continuously of ourselves and our pedagogies what the sources of our passions and desires are, what effects our passions and desires have on others, and in what ways our passions and desires might interface with desiring others in productive and unproductive ways" (130). I have explored how infrequently we really know the answer to Kelly's questions. Students infer truths about teachers' personal lives and desires in the classroom, and they come to know us in ways that we cannot know ourselves. Likewise, we come to know our students as we invite them to interact with us.

For any conversation to be meaningful, it should involve the entire person. It is not meaningful when we provide a canned or institutional voice in answer to a student's frustration or boredom or confusion. The classroom becomes meaningful to us when our students experience the whole person of the teacher and we experience theirs as well. We do not need to use the magic of the role to further our narcissistic aims, but we do need to remember that teaching is also about relationships. Our students want to know that we are human beings as well as teachers and that we recognize their humanity as well as their position as students. Staying within our assigned institutional roles can provide safety, distance, and predictability but not a lot of humanity in our classrooms. Leaving these roles can be very risky, but it is perhaps one of the most important risks that we can take.

In an exploration of how the analyst's subjectivity is experienced by the analytic patient, Lewis Aron notes that "patients seek to connect to their analysts, to know them, to probe beneath their professional façade, and to read their psychic centers in much the way that children seek to connect to and penetrate their parents' inner worlds" (29). Although it is with much less intensity, students often want to know about their teachers' inner lives as they seek to connect with them and the course material. A teacher's autobiographical revelations can open up the world of the classroom, inviting students to be the complex and multifaceted individuals that they are. When students learn, for example, that their teacher, who is a lover of elegant prose, is also a musician who puts on plastic gloves to protect her hands when she takes out the garbage, they might perceive that their teacher knows that they also have multiple aspects of themselves and that these aspects are welcome in the classroom. Similarly, a teacher who announces that she is a feminist and that there will be no sexist language in the classroom can prevent some of her students from transforming their learned sexism into a more tolerant acceptance. I remember being told of a graduate course in which "no racist or sexist language will be allowed" and an undergraduate course in which "no offensive language was permitted"; in neither, I suspect, did students feel invited into more fully human relationships with their teacher and with one another. When these statements are offered before any student has uttered a word, they can prevent the class from stumbling into and emerging together from the darkest places in human experiences.

Jerome Bruner suggests that "we carry with us habits of thought and taste fostered in some nearly forgotten classroom by a certain teacher" (24). He labels the "ordinary interactions" of classroom experience "folk pedagogy" and notes that it includes "the issue of how human beings achieve a meeting of minds, expressed by teachers as 'how do I reach [the students]? (46–47). Our students try to reach into our minds in all kinds of ways. Teachers who reveal personal details of their lives consciously play with and shape their subjectivities in front of their students by organizing the details of a life into a self before the class. Although we run the risk of making ourselves into the only text in the classroom when we tell our stories, if we choose those stories carefully, we also have opportunities to allow students to articulate something about who they are and who they might become, one moment at a time.

WORKS CITED

Angelo, Thomas A., and K. Patricia Cross. *Classroom Assessment Techniques.* 2nd ed. San Francisco: Jossey-Bass, 1993.

Anzaldúa, Gloria. "*La Conciencia de la Mestiza*/Towards a New Consciousness." In Colombo, Cullen, and Lisle, 434–43.

Aron, Lewis. "Clinical Choices and the Relational Matrix." *Psychoanalytic Dialogues* 9 (1999): 1–30.

———. "The Patient's Experiences of the Analyst's Subjectivity." *Psychoanalytic Dialogues* 1 (1991): 29–51.

Bartholomae, David. "Inventing the University." In *When a Writer Can't Write: Studies in Writer's Block and Other Composing Process Problems*, edited by Mike Rose, 134–65. New York: Guildord, 1985.

———. "A Reply to Stephen North." *PRE/TEXT* 11 (1990): 122–30.

Beebe, Beatrice, and Frank M. Lachmann. *Infant Research and Adult Treatment: Co-constructing Interactions.* Hillsdale, N.J.: Analytic Press, 2002.

Beebe, Beatrice, and Daniel Stern. "Engagement-Disengagement and Early Object Experiences." In *Communicative Structures and Psychic Structures*, edited by Norbert Freedman and Stanley Grand, 35–55. New York: Plenum Press, 1977.

Berman, Jeffrey. "Crying in the Classroom." *Chronicle of Higher Education*, 18 April 2003, 5.

———. *Diaries to an English Professor: Pain and Growth in the Classroom.* Amherst: University of Massachusetts Press, 1994.

Berthoff, Ann E. "Symposium: English 1999: Reclaiming the Active Mind." *College English* 61 (1999): 671–80.

Boler, Megan. *Feeling Power: Emotions and Education.* New York: Routledge, 1999.

Bordo, Susan. "Hunger as Ideology." In *Unbearable Weight: Feminism, Western Culture, and the Body*, 99–134. Berkeley: University of California Press, 1993.

Bracher, Mark. *The Writing Cure: Psychoanalysis, Composition, and the Aims of Education.* Carbondale: Southern Illinois University Press, 1999.

Branscombe, N. Amanda, Dixie Goswami, and Jeffrey Schwartz, eds. *Students Teaching, Teachers Learning.* Portsmouth, N.H.: Heinemann-Boynton/Cook, 1992.

Britzman, Deborah. *After-Education: Anna Freud, Melanie Klein, and Psychoanalytic Histories of Learning.* Albany: State University of New York Press, 2003.

———. "Between 'Lifting' and 'Accepting': Observations on the Work of Angst in Learning." In *Psychoanalysis and Pedagogy*, edited by Stephen Appel, 6–27. Westport, Conn.: Bergin and Garvey, 1999.

————. *Lost Subjects, Contested Objects: Toward a Psychoanalytic Inquiry of Learning.* Albany: State University of New York Press, 1998.

————. *Practice Makes Practice: A Critical Study of Learning to Teach.* Albany: State University of New York Press, 1991.

————. "Thoughts Awaiting Thinkers: Group Psychology and Educational Life." *International Journal of Leadership in Education: Theory and Practice* 2 (1999): 313–35.

Bromberg, Philip. "Standing in the Spaces: The Multiplicity of the Self and the Psychoanalytic Relationship." *Contemporary Psychoanalysis* 32 (1996): 509–35.

Brooke, Robert. "Lacan, Transference, and Writing Instruction." *College English* 49 (1987): 679–91.

Brookfield, Stephen. *The Skillful Teacher.* San Francisco: Jossey-Bass, 1990.

Brookfield, Stephen, and Stephen Preskill. *Discussion as a Way of Teaching: Tools and Techniques for Democratic Classrooms.* San Francisco: Jossey-Bass, 1999.

Bruner, Jerome. *Acts of Meaning.* Cambridge: Harvard University Press, 1990.

Busch, Fred. "In the Neighborhood: Aspects of a Good Interpretation and a Developmental Lag in Ego Psychology." *Journal of the American Psychoanalytic Association* 41 (1993): 151–78.

Cintron, Ralph. *Angels' Town: Chero Ways, Gang Life, and the Rhetorics of Everyday.* Boston: Beacon Press, 1998.

Coles, Nicholas, and Susan V. Wall. "Conflict and Power in the Reader-Responses of Adult Basic Writers." *College English* 49 (1987): 298–314.

Coles, Robert. "The Tradition: Fact or Fiction." In *Doing Documentary Work,* 87–145. New York: New York Public Library; New York: Oxford University Press, 1997.

Collins, Billy. "This Much I Do Remember." In *Picnic, Lightning,* 49. Pittsburgh: University of Pittsburgh Press, 1998.

Colombo, Gary, Robert Cullen, and Bonnie Lisle, eds. *Rereading America: Cultural Contexts for Critical Thinking and Writing.* 3rd ed. Boston: St. Martin's, Bedford, 1995.

Cooper, Stephen. "Facts All Come with a Point of View: Some Reflections on Fact and Formulation from the 75th Anniversary Edition of the International Journal of Psychoanalysis." *International Journal of Psychoanalysis* 77 (1996): 255–77.

————. *Objects of Hope: Exploring Possibility and Limit in Psychoanalysis.* Hillsdale, N.J.: Analytic Press, 2000.

Cottle, Thomas J. *A Sense of Self: The Work of Affirmation.* Amherst: University of Massachusetts Press, 2003.

Curzan, Anne, and Lisa Damour. *First Day to Final Grade: A Graduate Student's Guide to Teaching.* Ann Arbor: University of Michigan Press, 2000.

Cushman, Ellen. "The Public Intellectual, Service Learning, and Activist Research." *College English* 61 (1999): 328–36.

Duffy, Donna Killian, and Janet Wright Jones. *Teaching within the Rhythms of the Semester.* San Francisco: Jossey-Bass, 1995.

Elbow, Peter. *Embracing Contraries: Explorations in Learning and Teaching.* Oxford: Oxford University Press, 1986.

————. *Writing with Power: Techniques for Mastering the Writing Process.* 2nd ed. New York: Oxford University Press, 1998.

Eliot, T. S. "Love Song of J. Alfred Prufrock." *Poetry,* June 1915.

Faigley, Lester. "Competing Theories of Process: A Critique and a Proposal." *College English* 48 (1986): 527–41.

———. "Judging Writing, Judging Selves." *College Composition and Communication* 40 (1989): 395–412.

Felman, Shoshana. "Psychoanalysis and Education: Teaching Terminable and Interminable." *Yale French Studies* 63 (1982): 21–44.

Finke, Laurie. "Knowledge as Bait: Feminism, Voice, and the Pedagogical Unconscious." *College English* 55 (1993): 7–27.

Fleikenstein, Kristie S. "Writing Bodies: Somatic Mind in Composition Studies." *College English* 61 (1999): 281–306.

Foucault, Michel. The History of Sexuality: An Introduction. Translated by Robert Hurley. Vol. 1. New York: Random House, 1978; French, 1976.

Frankel, Jay. "Exploring Ferenczi's Concept of Identification with the Aggressor: Its Role in Trauma, Everyday Life, and the Therapeutic Relationship." *Psychoanalytic Dialogues* 12, no. 1 (2002): 101–40.

Freire, Paulo. *Pedagogy of the Oppressed*. New York: Seabury Press, 1973.

Freud, Sigmund. "The Dynamics of the Transference." In *Collected Papers*, translated by Joan Rivière, 2:312–22. London: Hogarth, 1949.

Fulkerson, Richard. "Call Me Horatio: Negotiating between Cognition and Affect in Composition." *College Composition and Communication* 50 (1998): 101–15.

Gabbard, Glen O. "An Overview of Countertransference: Theory and Technique." Chapter 3 in *Countertransference Issues*. Washington, D.C.: American Psychiatric Press, 1999.

Gardner, Howard. *Multiple Intelligences: The Theory in Practice*. New York: Basic, 1993.

Gendlin, Eugene T. *Focusing*. New York: Bantam, 1981.

Goleman, Daniel. *Emotional Intelligence: Why It Can Matter More Than IQ*. New York: Bantam, 1995.

Gottschalk, Katherine. *Facilitating Discussion: A Brief Guide*. Ithaca: Cornell University, 1994.

Greene, Maxine. *Releasing the Imagination: Essays on Education, the Arts, and Social Change*. San Francisco: Jossey-Bass, 2000.

Harris, Joseph. "After Dartmouth: Growth and Conflict in English." *College English* 53 (1991): 631–46.

Harris, Judith. *Signifying Pain: Constructing and Healing the Self through Writing*. Albany: State University of New York Press, 2003.

———. A Teaching Subject: Composition since 1966. Upper Saddle River, N.J.: Prentice Hall, 1997.

Heimann, Paula. "On Countertransference." *International Journal of Psychoanalysis* 31 (1950): 81–84.

Henderson, Mae Gwendolyn. "Speaking in Tongues: Dialogics, Dialectics, and the Black Woman Writer's Literary Tradition." In *Changing Our Own Words: Essays on Criticism, Theory, and Writing by Black Women*, edited by Cheryl Wall, 16–37. New Brunswick, N.J.: Rutgers University Press, 1989.

Herrington, Anne. *Persons in Process: Four Stories of Writing and Personal Development in College*. Urbana, Ill.: National Council of Teachers of English, 2000.

Herzog, James M. *Father Hunger: Explorations with Adults and Children*. Hillsdale, N.J.: Analytic Press, 2001.

Hesse, Doug. "Saving a Place for Essayistic Literacy." In *Passions, Pedagogies, and 21st Century Technologies*, edited by Gail E. Hawisher and Cynthia E. Selfe, 34–48. Logan: University of Utah Press; Urbana, Ill.: National Council of Teachers of English, 1999.

Hoffman, Irwin Z. *Ritual and Spontaneity in the Psychoanalytic Process: A Dialectical-Constructivist View*. Hillsdale, N.J.: Analytic Press, 1998.

Holland, Norman. "The New Paradigm: Subjective or Transactive?" *New Literary History: A Journal of Theory and Interpretation* 7 (1976): 335–46.

Holland, Norman, and Murray Schwartz. "The Delphi Seminar." *College English* 36 (1975): 789–800.

Jacobs, Dale, and Laura R. Micciche, eds. *A Way to Move: Rhetorics of Emotion and Composition Studies*. CrossCurrents: New Perspectives in Rhetoric and Composition Series. Portsmouth, N.H.: Boynton/Cook, 2003.

Jacobs, Theodore. "On the Question of Self-Disclosure by the Analyst: Error or Advance in Technique?" *Psychoanalytic Quarterly* 68 (1999): 159–83.

James, William. *On Some of Life's Ideals: On a Certain Blindness in Human Beings; What Makes Life Significant*. New York: Henry Holt and Company, [1900].

Jay, Gregory S. "The Subject of Pedagogy: Lessons in Psychoanalysis and Politics." *College English* 49 (1987): 785–800.

Johnson, T. R. *A Rhetoric of Pleasure: Prose Style and Today's Composition Classroom*. Portsmouth, N.H.: Heinemann-Boynton/Cook, 2003.

———. "School Sucks." *College Composition and Communication* 54 (2001): 620–50.

Keats, John. *Letters of John Keats*. Edited by Robert Gittings. Oxford: Oxford University Press, 1970.

Kelly, Ursula. *Schooling Desire: Literacy, Cultural Politics, and Pedagogy*. New York: Routledge, 1997.

Kennedy, X. J., Dorothy M. Kennedy, and Sylvia A. Holladay. *The Bedford Guide for College Writers*. 6th ed. Boston: St. Martins, Bedford, 2002.

Kernberg, Otto. "Thirty Methods to Destroy the Creativity of Psychoanalytic Candidates." *International Journal of Psychoanalysis* 77 (1996): 1031–40.

Kincaid, Jamaica. "Girl." In Colombo, Cullen, and Lisle, 241–43.

Kirsner, Douglas. "The Radical Edge." Paper presented at the annual meeting of the San Francisco Psychoanalytic Institute, San Francisco, 1996.

Krakauer, Jon. *Into the Wild*. New York: Anchor, 1997.

Kris, Anton O. "Interpretation and the Method of Free Association." *Psychoanalytic Inquiry* 12 (1992): 208–24.

Lindemann, Erika. *A Rhetoric for Writing Teachers*. 3rd ed. New York: Oxford University Press, 2001.

Lu, Min-Zhan. "Conflict and Struggle: The Enemies or Preconditions of Basic Writing?" *College English* 54 (1992): 887–913.

Lyons-Ruth, Karlen. "The Two-Person Construction of Defenses: Disorganized Attachment Strategies, Unintegrated Mental States, and Hostile/-Helpless

Relational Process." *Newsletter of the Division on Psychoanalytic Psychology of the American Psychological Association*, 2001, 2–3.

McGee, Patrick. "Truth and Resistance: Teaching as a Form of Analysis." *College English* 49 (1987): 667–78.

McKeachie, Wilbert J. *McKeachie's Teaching Tips: Strategies, Research, and Theory for College and University Teachers*. Boston: Houghton Mifflin, 1999.

Miller, Richard E. "The Arts of Complicity: Pragmatism and the Culture of Schooling." *College English* 61 (1998): 10–28.

———. *As If Learning Mattered: Reforming Higher Education*. Ithaca: Cornell University Press, 1998.

———. "Fault Lines in the Contact Zone." *College English* 56 (1994): 389–408.

Mitchell, Stephen A. *Hope and Dread in Psychoanalysis*. New York: Basic, 1995.

Mukherjee, Bharati. *Jasmine*. New York: Grove Press, 1989.

Murphy, Ann. "Transference and Resistance in the Basic Writing Classroom." *College Composition and Communication* 40 (1989): 175–88.

Murray, Donald. "The Listening Eye: Reflections on the Writing Conference." In *The Writing Teacher's Sourcebook*, edited by E. P. J. Corbett, N. Myers, and G. Tate, 66–71. 4th ed. New York: Oxford University Press, 2000.

———. "Teaching the Other Self: The Writer's First Reader." In *Composition in Four Keys: Inquiring into the Field; Art, Nature, Science, Politics*, edited by Mark Wiley, Barbara Gleason, and Louise Wetherbee Phelps, 50–55. Mountain View, Calif.: Mayfield Publishing, 1996.

———. "Teach Writing as a Process Not a Product." In *Cross-Talk in Comp Theory: A Reader*, edited by Victor Villanueva Jr., 3–6. Urbana, Ill.: National Council of Teachers of English, 1999.

———. *A Writer Teaches Writing*. Boston: Houghton Mifflin, 1985.

Newkirk, Thomas. *The Performance of Self in Student Writing*. Portsmouth, N.H.: Heinemann-Boynton/Cook, 1997.

Ogden, Thomas. *Projective Identification and Psychotherapeutic Technique*. New York: J. Aronson, 1982.

Ong, Walter J. "Literacy and Orality in Our Times." *ADE Bulletin* 58 (1978): 1–7.

Palmer, Parker. *The Courage to Teach*. San Francisco: Jossey-Bass, 1998.

Perl, Sondra. "Understanding Composing." In *The Writing Teacher's Sourcebook*, edited by Gary Tate, Edward P. J. Corbett, and Nancy Myers, 149–54. 3rd ed. New York: Oxford University Press, 1994.

Peterson, Linda. "Gender and the Autobiographical Essay: Research Perspectives, Pedagogical Practices." *College Composition and Communication* 42 (1981): 171–83.

Power, Dolan. "A Consideration of Knowledge and Authority in the Case Seminar." *Psychoanalytic Quarterly* 70 (2001): 625–53.

Pratt, Mary Louise. "Arts of the Contact Zone." In *Professing in the Contact Zone: Bringing Theory and Practice Together*, edited by Janice M. Wolff, 1–18. Urbana, Ill.: National Council of Teachers of English, 2002.

Prendergast, Catherine. "Race: The Absent Presence in Composition Studies." *College Composition and Communication* 50, no. 1 (1998): 36–53.

Prufrock, J. Alfred. "Love Song of J. Alfred Prufrock." *Poetry*, June 1915.

Rankin, Elizabeth Deane. *Seeing Yourself as a Teacher: Conversations with Five New Teachers in a University Writing Program*. Urbana, Ill.: National Council of Teachers of English, 1994.

Reik, Theodor. *Listening with the Third Ear: The Inner Experience of a Psychoanalyst*. New York: Farrar, Strauss, 1948.

Renik, Owen. "The Ideal of the Anonymous Analyst and the Problem of Self-Disclosure." *Psychoanalytic Quarterly* 64 (1995): 466–95.

———. "On the Perils of Neutrality." *Psychoanalytic Quarterly* 65 (1996): 495–517.

Rich, Adrienne. "Notes towards a Politics of Location." In *Blood, Bread, and Poetry: Selected Prose, 1979–1985*, 210–31. New York: Norton, 1986.

———. "Vesuvius at Home: The Power of Emily Dickinson." In *On Lies, Secrets, and Silence: Selected Prose, 1966–1978*, 151–83. New York: Norton, 1979.

———. "When We Dead Awaken: Writing as Re-Vision." In *On Lies, Secrets, and Silence: Selected Prose, 1966–1978*, 33–49. New York: Norton, 1979.

Rodriguez, Richard. "The Achievement of Desire." In *Hunger of Memory: The Education of Richard Rodriguez; An Autobiography*, 41–74. Boston: D. R. Godine, 1982.

Rosendale, Laura Gray. "Cracks in the Contact Zone." In *Questioning Authority: Stories Told in School*, edited by Linda Adler-Kassner and Susanmarie Harrington, 153–67. Ann Arbor: University of Michigan Press, 2001.

Roskelly, Hephzibah, and Kate Ronald. *Reason to Believe: Romanticism, Pragmatism, and the Teaching of Writing*. New York: State University of New York Press, 1998.

Rouzie, Albert. "Conversation and Carrying-on: Play, Conflict, and Serio-Ludic Discourse in Computer Conferencing." *College Composition and Communication* 53 (2001): 251–99.

Sander, Louis W. "The Regulation of Exchange in the Infant Caretaker System and Some Aspects of the Context-Content Relationship." In *Interaction, Conversation, and the Development of Language*, edited by Michael Lewis and L. Rosenblum, 133–56. New York: Wiley, 1977.

———. "Thinking Differently: Principles of Process in Living Systems and the Specificity of Being Known." *Psychoanalytic Dialogues* 12 (2002): 11–42.

Sandler, Joseph. "Countertransference and Role-Responsiveness." *International Review of Psychoanalysis* 3 (1976): 43–47.

Schank, Roger C., and John B. Cleave. "Natural Learning, Natural Teaching." In *The Mind, the Brain, and Complex Adaptive Systems*, edited by Harold Morowitz and Jerome L. Singer, 175–202. Santa Fe Institute Studies in the Sciences of Complexity, Proceedings 22. Reading, Mass.: Addison-Wesley, 1995.

Schön, Donald A. *Educating the Reflective Practitioner: Toward a New Design for Teaching and Learning in the Professions*. San Francisco: Jossey-Bass, 1988.

Schweickart, Patrocinio. "Reading Ourselves: Toward a Feminist Theory of Reading." In *Feminisms: An Anthology of Literary Theory and Criticism*, edited by Robyn R. Warhol and Diane Price Herndl, 525–50. New Brunswick, N.J.: Rutgers University Press, 1991.

Smith, Henry F. "Analytic Listening and the Experience of Surprise." *International Journal of Psychoanalysis* 76 (1995): 67–78.

Sommer, Doris. "'Not Just a Personal Story': Women's *Testimonios* and the Plural Self." In *Writing Women's Lives: An Anthology of Autobiographical Narratives by Twentieth Century Women Writers*, edited by Susan Cahill, 107–30. New York: HarperPerennial, 1994.

Sommers, Nancy. "Responding to Student Writing." *College Composition and Communication* 33 (1982): 148–56.

Sorenson, Randall. "Psychoanalytic Institutes as Religious Denominations: Fundamentalism, Progeny, and Ongoing Reformation." *Psychoanalytic Dialogues* 10 (2000): 847–74.

Spellmeyer, Kurt. "After Theory: From Textuality to Attunement with the World." *College English* 58 (1996): 893–913.

———. *Common Ground: Dialogue, Understanding, and the Teaching of Composition.* Englewood Cliffs, N.J.: Prentice Hall, 1993.

Stechler, Gerald. "Louis W. Sander and the Question of Affective Presence." *Infant Mental Health* 21 (2000): 75–84.

Stern, Daniel. *The Interpersonal World of the Infant.* New York: Basic, 1985.

Stern, Daniel, et al. "Non-Interpretive Mechanisms in Psychoanalytic Therapy: The 'Something More' Than Interpretation." *International Journal of Psychoanalysis* 79 (1998): 903–21.

Sternglass, Marilyn. *Time to Know Them: A Longitudinal Study of Writing and Learning at the College Level.* Mahway, N.J.: Lawrence Erlbaum Associates, 1997.

Stevens, Wallace. "The Poems of Our Climate." In *The Collected Poems of Wallace Stevens*, 193. New York: Knopf, 1999.

Stolorow, Robert. "Dynamic, Dyadic, Intersubjective Systems: An Evolving Paradigm for Psychoanalysis." *Psychoanalytic Psychology* 14 (1997): 337–46.

———. "Principles of Psychoanalytic Exploration." In *Psychoanalytic Treatment: An Intersubjective Approach*, 1–14. Hillsdale, N.J.: Analytic Press, 1987.

Stolorow, Robert, and George Atwood. *Faces in a Cloud: Subjectivity in Personality Theory.* Northvale, N.J.: Jason Aronson, 1979.

———. *Structures of Subjectivity: Explorations in Psychoanalytic Phenomenology.* Hillsdale, N.J.: Analytic Press, 1984.

Street, Brian. *Social Literacies: Critical Approaches to Literacy in Development, Ethnography, and Education.* London: Longman, 1995.

Tannen, Deborah. "The Roots of Debate in Education and the Hope of Dialogue." In *The Argument Culture: Moving from Debate to Dialogue*, 255–90. New York: Ballantine, 1999.

Thelen, Esther, and Linda B. Smith. *A Dynamic Systems Approach to the Development of Cognition and Action.* Cambridge: MIT Press, 1994.

Tiberius, Richard G., and Jane Tipping. "The Discussion Leader: Fostering Student Learning in Groups." In *Teaching Alone, Teaching Together: Transforming the Structure of Teams for Teaching*, edited by James L. Bess and associates, 108–30. San Francisco: Jossey-Bass, 2000.

Tobin, Lad. *Writing Relationships: What Really Happens in the Composition Class*. Portsmouth, N.H.: Heinemann-Boynton/Cook, 1993.

Tompkins, Jane. *A Life in School: What the Teacher Learned*. Reading, Mass.: Addison-Wesley, 1996.

Trimmer, Joseph F. *Narration as Knowledge: Tales of the Teaching Life*. Portsmouth, N.H.: Heinemann-Boynton/Cook, 1997.

Tronick, Edward Z. "'Of Course All Relationships Are Unique': How Co-creative Processes Generate Unique Mother-Infant and Patient-Therapist Relationships and Change Other Relationships." *Psychoanalytic Inquiry* 23 (2003): 473–91.

Tronick, Edward Z., et al. "Dyadically Expanded States of Consciousness and the Process of Therapeutic Change." *Infant Mental Health Journal* 19 (1998): 290–99.

Walker, Alice. "Beauty: When the Other Dancer Is the Self." In *Fields of Writing: Readings across the Disciplines*. 4th ed. Edited by Nancy Comley et al., 46–53. New York: St. Martin's, 1994.

Waters, Anne. "Reaching In and Out with Gerry Stechler." *Free Associations* 4, no. 1 (2003): 2, 7.

Welch, Cyril. "Talking." *Philosophy and Rhetoric* 18 (1985): 216–35.

Wikan, Unni. *Managing Turbulent Hearts: A Balinese Formula for Living*. Chicago: University of Chicago Press, 1990.

Williams, Joseph M. "The Phenomenology of Error." *College Composition and Communication* 32 (1981): 152–68, 239.

Winnicott, Donald W. *The Maturational Process and the Facilitating Environment*. New York: International University Press, 1965.

———. *Playing and Reality*. New York: Tavistock, 1971.

Woolf, Virginia. *Moments of Being: Unpublished Autobiographical Writings*. Edited, with an introduction and notes, by Jeanne Schulkind. London: Chatto and Windus for Sussex University Press, 1976.

Wordsworth, William. *The Complete Poetical Works of William Wordsworth*. London: Macmillan, 1888.

Dawn M. Skorczewski was born in Elmira, New York. She holds a B.A. from Boston College and a Ph.D. from Rutgers University. She has been a Silberger Scholar at the Boston Psychoanalytic Institute, and is currently on the faculty of the Massachusetts Psychoanalytic Institute and of the Cincinnati Psychoanalytic Institute. She is Associate Professor of English and Director of University Writing at Brandeis University. She has also served as Director of Composition at the University of Redlands and Emerson College. She lives in Cambridge, Massachusetts.